Day Trading

A Detailed Guide on Day Trading Strategies

(Easy Introduction to Making Money While Managing Your Risk)

Charles Loughran

Published By **John Kembrey**

Charles Loughran

Day Trading: A Detailed Guide on Day Trading Strategies (Easy Introduction to Making Money While Managing Your Risk)

ISBN   978-1-998927-43-2

No part of this guidebook shall be reproduced in any form without permission in writing from the publisher except in the case of brief quotations embodied in critical articles or reviews.

Legal & Disclaimer

The information contained in this book is not designed to replace or take the place of any form of medicine or professional medical advice. The information in this book has been provided for educational & entertainment purposes only.

The information contained in this book has been compiled from sources deemed reliable, and it is accurate to the best of the Author's knowledge; however, the Author cannot guarantee its accuracy and validity and cannot be held liable for any errors or omissions. Changes are periodically made to this book. You must consult your doctor or get professional medical advice before using any of the suggested remedies, techniques, or information in this book.

Table Of Contents

Chapter 1: How To Use The Economic Calendar 1

Chapter 2: Economic News That Matters For The Usd... 9

Chapter 3: Economic News That Matters For The Gbp 18

Chapter 4: Bank Of Japanwhat To Know When Trading The Jpy............................. 25

Chapter 5: What Matters For The Euro .. 31

Chapter 6: Ecb And Its Mandate 35

Chapter 7: Federal Reserve Of The Usastructure, Mandate, Role 38

Chapter 8: What Matters For The Aussie Dollar 43

Chapter 9: Bank Of Canada And The Loonie Dollar 51

Chapter 10: Interpreting The Housing Data In The United States............................... 55

Chapter 11: Bank Of England And Its Role At The Pound's Fluctuation 59

Chapter 12: News Trading Vs. Technical Trading.. 62

Chapter 13: Macroeconomicshow Investing Starts 68

Chapter 14: Explaining Forward Guidance 71

Chapter 15: Deflation Vs. Inflationhow To Fight Them... 75

Chapter 16: Hyperinflation Or What Happens When Money Dies................... 80

Chapter 17: Setting Up Your Equipment 87

Chapter 18: Learn The Important Rules . 93

Chapter 19: Open Your Brokerage Account 100

Chapter 20: Stop-Loss And Take-Earnings 108

Chapter 21: Study Your Stocks 115

Chapter 22: Develop Your Trading Plan 118

Chapter 23: Start Paper Trading........... 124

Chapter 24: The Basics Of Trading 137

Chapter 25: Basic And Investment
Strategies.. 146

Chapter 26: How To Develop Your Own
Strategy 152

Chapter 27: Ideal Tools And Software.. 162

Chapter 28: Do-It-Yourself Risks........... 172

Chapter 1: How To Use The Economic Calendar

This part of our collection dedicated to foreign exchange deals with essential evaluation thoughts which might be required knowledge for each retail issuer. Central banks and their respective monetary hints rely the maximum in foreign exchange and, besides the retail trader is conscious what drives modifications in the fundamentals, achieving achievement in shopping for and promoting is probably hard.

We've already protected a few crucial assessment mind in preceding books of our series. But proper here we shift cognizance to essential banking, investing, macroeconomics, and exceptional elements (besides technical evaluation, of path) that the provider needs to don't forget.

For the retail provider, there's a sturdy temptation to best use technical symptoms, such as oscillators and extremely good trading theories, to forecast future expenses. But it is said that at the identical time as technical evaluation gives the market's path, the market movements for a reason. Working out why the market actions: that is essential assessment.

The the Forex market dashboard is commonplace with the aid of foreign exchange pairs that flow into towards every awesome. Besides the usage of technical evaluation, buyers interpret the financial releases for each usa of the us of the us and alternate the currencies based totally on their evaluation.

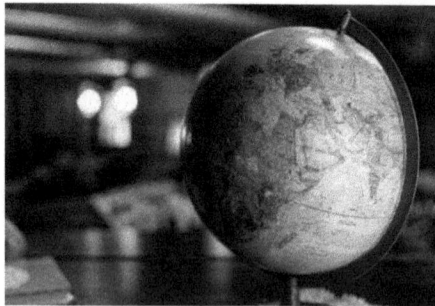

So, we're capable to mention that shopping for and promoting based mostly on crucial analysis is mostly a depend of decoding economic facts. Some customers handiest use financial records because the idea for their buying and selling-associated choices.

The concept is to compare monetary releases from particular international locations and decide which one is acting higher. Based on the final results of the comparisons, investors buy or sell a foreign exchange or a foreign cash pair.

The location to get financial information and be prepared for market's volatility is the financial calendar. No purchasing for and promoting have to take location if the issuer doesn't understand what monetary release is up subsequent, what forex is going to be affected, and what the forecast is.

Remember that essential analysis gives the motive why the market moves? The economic calendar will let you comprehend why and while the market will circulate.

For instance, if the NFP (Non-Farm Payrolls) is due to pop out, the market really gained't bypass till its release. Consulting the economic calendar is a exquisite way to tune the marketplace timing and to prepare for the volatility spikes to comply with.

The "economic calendar" is a basket of free records critical for actually absolutely everyone interested by buying and selling the foreign cash marketplace. A simple Internet are seeking for reveals many net sites that offer the information and the data is break up into three classes:

- Third-tier records

•This is financial statistics that doesn't in fact flow into the markets. Its characteristic is to supplement the possibility financial releases just so the traders can shape a whole photo of an economic gadget. Typically, for the financial calendars that use a coloration code to consciousness at the records' significance, the statistics belonging to this elegance comes within the coloration yellow, related to non-marketplace-moving facts.

- Second-tier facts

•Marked with the colour orange, 2d-tier information has the capability to transport the market. Examples of such releases are the Durable Goods within the United States or housing statistics anywhere in the global. These are extraordinarily crucial, in particular if the real numbers range a incredible deal from the forecast.

- First-tier records

•This is in which each supplier's reputation need to be. Marked with the colour pink, those monetary releases check with vital facts for a overseas money or foreign exchange pair:

o Inflation

o Unemployment price

o Consumer spending

o Retail earnings

o GDPGross Domestic Product

o Jobs records

o PMI's

For each release, the financial calendar suggests the preceding release final outcomes, the forecast, and the real. Using those, a elegant interpretation tells the supplier what the marketplace should do relying on how the real launch compares with the forecast.

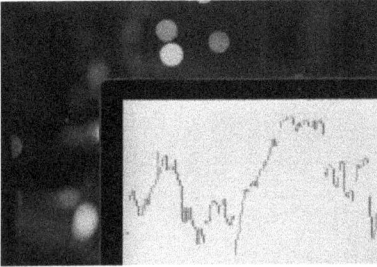

If we use the unemployment price for example: the lower it's far, the better for the monetary device. A low unemployment price shows excessive employment degrees, and an increasing financial gadget. So, suitable for the financial machine and for the foreign exchange. If the unemployment charge comes out better than expectations (the actual lower than forecast), customers will interpret it as bullish for the foreign cash and will move lengthy.

On pinnacle of that, the financial calendar gives access to historic facts as well, virtually so analytical investors can gather fashions to appearance how the economic device is appearing now whilst in evaluation with historical tiers.

One manner to stay up to date with what's taking region is to constantly consult the financial calendar at the start of the trading week to see what data has the capability to effect the markets next. This way, clients can modify the objectives for his or her trades in addition to enhance their timing.

Chapter 2: Economic News That Matters For The Usd

With the Bretton Woods agreement, the U.S. Dollar took center stage as the arena's reserve overseas coins. It changed the GBP (Great Britain Pound) and function grow to be the foreign exchange of choice whilst undertaking global change and the one utilized by sovereign worldwide locations to build up reserves.

It have become even extra important whilst the Nixon manage decided to scrap the gold present day inside the early 1970s. From that second on, the price of any given foreign money began out to depend an extended way extra intently on the behavior of relevant banking in the United States and distinct capitalistic economies. .

A new marketplace became born, wherein mainly institutional customers ought to speculate on the loose-floating currencies. Soon, the Internet and private computer systems regarded, and retail customers acquired access to the interbank marketplace at the same time as brokerage homes offered access to it for a fee or fee.

Throughout all this, the U.S. Dollar's characteristic elevated in significance. A large bite of global flows, further to coins deliver maintained out of doors of the united states, makes the dollar the favored preference to accumulate reserves international.

Even the the Forex market dashboard as we recognize it these daysas we've discussed inside the preceding books in our collectionis focused across the greenback.

Depending at the greenback's presence in a distant places money pair, it's considered every a major or a pass. The U.S. Dollar is the pillar of the modern-day-day economic gadget and holds together the Forex dashboard.

There's a saying among retail the Forex market customers that during case you recognize the dollar's direction, you realize in which all the different forex pairs will journey subsequent. And what drives the dollar is particularly the economic news out of the us.

As the maximum important economic system in the international, it's miles no wonder that what takes region within the United States affects the worldwide monetary device. So, if there's one economic device to have a look at from a essential evaluation aspect of view while buying and selling the overseas cash market, it's the US monetary system.

Besides the hobby fee alternatives and regular monetary insurance bulletins and speeches, there's a plethora of monetary data out of the usa that remember wide variety for the greenback.

Inflation, or the CPI (Consumer Price Index), tops the listing. It refers back to the trade in fees of goods and offerings in the United States financial gadget over a particular duration.

Typically released monthly, it's miles the statistics taken into consideration via the Fed at the same time as assessing the charge balance inside the economic machine. As a tip for retail Forex customers, the Fed specializes in the "middle" launch, in area of the conventional CPI.

The Core CPI data doesn't don't forget strength prices due to their inherent volatility. The charge of oil has a large impact at the inflationary outlook, and from time to time it's far distinctly transitory.

For this purpose, many treasured banks neglect about it and interest on the middle data. Another tip to keep in mind at the same time as searching at inflation is to be aware about the PPI release as nicely. The PPI stands for Producers Price Index, and it represents inflation at the manufacturers' component.

The traditional attention is that changes within the PPI are in the long run pondered within the CPI, that is why savvy buyers watch the PPI. They'll have a caution about in which the CPI is going to move.

Jobs records is 2d in line in terms of importance. Like inflation, jobs introduction is a critical part of the Fed's mandate.

Several jobs related releases provide clues to traders approximately what the Fed will do next with the prices. NFP (Non-Farm Payrolls) tops the list and is one of the key measures that the Fed considers together with inflation.

The NFP comes out each first Friday of each month and the rate movement at a few level in the NFP week is marked via tight stages. Together with the NFP, the Unemployment Rate fills out the jobs information image and helps shoppers prepare for the subsequent decision regarding the federal price range fee.

Earlier in that identical week, on Wednesday, the ADP, or personal payrolls shows the dominion of the private vicinity. Traders use this launch as a strong indicator for wherein the NFP will detail, but there can be no examined correlation between the ADP and NFP.

Initial Jobless Claims and Continuing Claims entire the jobs picture. Many buyers view those as redundant, however the pop out weekly on Thursdays, and they do offer a glimpse into the NFP records.

The ISM releases are to be had in a close to 1/3 vicinity. The same of PMI's within the rest of the area, the ISM's call comes from the entity that calculates the fee: the Institute for Supply Management.

The ISM has versions, every one regarding a terrific region within the United States monetary machine: ISM Manufacturing and ISM Non-Manufacturing. Because the united states economic system is company-based virtually, the Non-Manufacturing (a.Okay.A.

Services   corporation)   release   is   extra

applicable for the high-quality interpretation
of the monetary u . S . A ..

One interesting factor approximately the ISM
facts   is   that   consumers/marketplace
participants interpret it relative to the 50
stage. Any factor above this degree suggests
an growing financial system and builds a
hawkish case for the Fed and a bullish
situation for the dealer.

On the alternative hand, a dip underneath the
50 mark indicates a region and possibly an
monetary   gadget   that   shrinks   into
recessionary territory and the Fed will begin
easing financial insurance.

Besides the headline (the actual range), the
ISM   releases   an   in   depth   report

approximately the economic stance of every of the two sectors. For foreign exchange buyers searching out to anticipate the following rate alternate from the Fed, make certain to test that unique file and no longer genuinely the headline.

Savvy investors use this possibility to check the employment hassle of every the producing and non-manufacturing sectors. Because at the least one of the ISM releases (and in some months each of them) pop out in advance than the NFP, traders use the employment element to expect the subsequent NFP amount.

Besides the ISM, popular, fashionable economic records actions the dollar too. Retail Sales, GDP, AHE (Average Hourly Earnings), Durable Goods, Housing Data, Consumer Confidence, are just a few properly sincerely worth thinking about.

Even on the financial calendar now not all of them are marked purple, certainly to trouble out the fact that a number of them are secondary in significance on the subject of transferring the market.

Because the enormously ultra-modern monetary crisis within the United States come to be due to the housing region, we've dedicated a totally unique chapter to it later in this ebook. So make certain you keep studying!

Chapter 3: Economic News That Matters For The Gbp

One of the opportunity key currencies that makes up the Forex dashboard, the GBP (Great Britain Pound) changed into as soon because the arena's reserve overseas cash earlier than the U.S. Dollar's dominance. It has an extended facts due to the fact the British Empire ruled the sector for quite some time.

The Bank of England, because the GBP mother or father, is one of the oldest treasured banks within the international. It plays a important function inside the GBP's valuation as it units the economic coverage for one of the most influential currencies within the free global.

The United Kingdom and the GBP have loved a unique repute inside the final years. While a part of the European Union, the UK chose to hold its personal overseas cash, and not to be a part of the Eurozone.

For years, the 2 currencies (EUR and GBP) unfastened-floated on the interbank marketplace and the remote places cash pairs they will be part of are unstable enough to attract buyers of all type.

From the begin, we'd upload that the GBP is a

miles more risky foreign exchange than others, even greater than the USD!

Pairs collectively with GBPCHF or GBPUSD have an ATR (Average True Range) plenty large than pairs which consist of EURUSD or AUDUSD, making them an appealing opportunity to investors spherical the arena that have particular techniques to approach the marketplace.

Now that the Brexit has end up a truth (in June 2016 the United Kingdom held a referendum to leave the European Union), the GBP and the U.K. Financial machine deserve precise interest. In fact, buying and promoting the GBP pairs in the and a 1/2 years that accompanied the Brexit vote have grow to be data-mounted and a hard challenge.

The United Kingdom's financial device is a unique one. Dependent on offerings, it's presently struggling to maintain worldwide agency, after the referendum.

London continues to be the sector's largest monetary district, with clearing charges outpacing even New York, now not to mention Tokyo and exceptional centers. The city of London stays iconic within the trading enterprise and generates a massive chew of the dominion's GDP.

For this reason, one of the most anticipated releases is the PMI Services. PMI stands for Purchasing Managers Index and is much like the ISM inside the United States we certainly mentioned in advance on this book.

In the U.K. The PMI is available in three exceptional releases, for three separate sectors:

- services

- manufacturing

- creation

Traders pay close to interest to the PMI Services launch. If the offerings vicinity suffers, the complete monetary device suffers.

The PMIs are interpreted primarily based definitely completely at the 50 stage, so anything above that diploma is right statistics. However, numbers too an prolonged manner above 50, i.E., sixty one or higher, is indicative of an overheating economic machine, and the critical monetary group can be expected to in the end intervene to exchange the financial coverage to cool subjects down.

For the PMIs the identical old interpretation is that if the PMI beats expectations, the pound will rise. And in turn, a decrease than predicted PMI release will grow to be with a lower pound all through the the Forex market dashboard.

The three sectors have unique weight at the GDP, so it's far vital to understand which one is most applicable. For example, it is able to be that the PMI Manufacturing launch disappoints, however so long as the PMI Services but comes out at the robust component, the GBP will shrug off any functionality susceptible factor.

Inflation, of path, topics while buying and selling the GBP pairs. The CPI (Consumer Price Index) launch creates heightened volatility at the GBP pairs, with the vital monetary group having the equal motive as all capitalistic economies: to hold inflation underneath or close to percentage.

What's exciting and specific is the Inflation Letter in the United Kingdom. It merits specific hobby due to the truth Forex customers managing the GBP pairs want to recognize whilst it comes out and why.

When inflation deviates from the intention with the resource of a couple of percentage, the BOE (Bank of England)'s Governor is needed to ship an open letter to the Chancellor, explaining why this is taking location and what the answers are for the destiny.

Even greater important is that the Inflation Letter launch is placed by using manner of way of a press conference wherein the BOE's Governor solutions questions from press representatives. Needless to say, the feedback create immoderate volatility at the GBP pairs and possibilities for the speculative retail trader.

The GDP suggests the complete fee of all the products and offerings created through the U.K. Financial machine. It comes out in diverse releases, and the maximum applicable one is the Preliminary GDP. The Secondary launch now not often differs from the primary one, and due to this, it's far generally discounted.

The Claimant Count and the Unemployment Rate every display the united states of the manner market in the country. The decrease they may be, the better for the British Pound, and the Forex market is the number one one to react to any variations some of the real and forecast numbers.

Chapter 4: Bank Of Japanwhat To Know When Trading The Jpy

With an emblematic monetary machine, Japan is a miracle of this international. Ruined after World War Two, it rose like a phoenix from ashes to turn out to be the second one largest economic device within the global.,

Despite its achievement, however, Japan struggles with a extremely-present day problem, one some distance huge and hard to

resolve: demography.

With the oldest energetic population in the worldwide, Japan faces a difficult monetary time. The hassle with the developing vintage population is that the humans don't spend as a lot coins anymore as they used to do in their more younger years.

JpegMoreover, the more youthful families pick out no longer to have kids or to have fewer than older generations did, developing a scarcity of people to update the lively personnel. Obviously, the monetary system have become first to look the effect and the issues contemplated to the overseas coins, the Japanese Yen, as properly.

BOJ (Bank of Japan) become the primary one to perceive the hassle on the horizon. As inflation dipped into awful territory, intake decreased at an alarming price.

When the consumer doesn't spend anymore, or spending decreases, a vicious economic circle paperwork. Retailers don't sell that hundreds anymore, so stock levels rise. As a final results, fewer orders are positioned to wholesalers.

Wholesalers see their inventories growing as nicely, in order that they'll lessen orders positioned with producers. At the prevent of this supply chain, the producers will ought to lay off humans and, as a stop end result, the unemployment rate for the authorities will upward push.

As a end end result, no one is satisfied: the populace (high unemployment effects in riots, discontent, and masses of others.) or the government (deficits will rise, better fees, hard to apprehend budgets, and so on.).

These are deflationary outcomes, what takes place at the equal time as inflation drops below zero. Or, more precisely, at the same time as the prices of merchandise and offerings drop.

To counter deflation and decrease inflation, BOJ used everything in its energy inside the last few a long time. Remember that the applicable economic group has the identical inflationary purpose: below or near percent.

It ran and however runs a huge quantitative easing software. Such packages, inspired with the resource of comparable programs inside the United States, had been designed to preserve inflation again to aim, similar to it took place in the States whilst Bernanke's Fed ran 4 separate quantitative easing programs in a row.

As it have become out, inflation within the States rose to intention, but it's though falling quick in Japan. Bank of Japan but runs the QE (searching for JGB'sJapanese Government Bonds) with the desire that inflation will upward push to purpose.

As a cease result of all this, inflation is the most important economic release to maintain in mind while looking at JPY pairs. Bank of Japan will do some thing in its electricity to carry it once more to goal, no matter the reality that that shows a complete distortion of the Japanese fixed earnings marketplace.

After inflation, the Tankan file is the subsequent in line to have an effect on the charge of the JPY. It is a comprehensive report outlining the general state of affairs of economic interest in Japan, containing a detailed rationalization of the way the financial gadget is doing at that one element in time.

Traders have a study the employment thing in particular and primary all exclusive info that would offer a clue concerning what the Bank of Japan will do next with the hobby rate levels for the JPY.

Perhaps the most crucial characteristic of the JPY and Bank of Japan's financial coverage is the indirect correlation it has with the global inventory market and, mainly, with the US inventory marketplace.

Because of the BOJ's efforts to convey inflation to goal, the JPY loved low interest charge ranges for quite some time. When shoppers search for better yields and decide to try and get them inside the stock marketplace, they search for cash to borrow for purchasing and promoting capital or to invest.

Naturally, they'll appearance to borrow in a overseas coins that bears the bottom hobby charge feasible. For pretty a long term that has been the JPY.

JpegSo, consumers borrow in JPY to buy USD to pay for U.S. Stocks. This creates a exquisite go with the go with the flow at the USDJPY pair, the maximum liquid JPY pair on the Forex dashboard.

Chapter 5: What Matters For The Euro

The Euro (EUR) is the forex of 19 European states that shape the Eurozone. For those human beings not familiar with how Europe is prepared, the Eurozone and the European Union are incredible matters.

Not all international locations which might be part of the European Union have the EUR as their foreign exchange. Only nineteen do.

The Euro grow to be born due to the fact the pillar of the European Union (E.U.) and has a great tale. The European Monetary System have turn out to be born inside the middle of the '70s, and the Euro as a prison clean regarded multiple a few years later after the Plaza Accord and the Maastricht Treaty.,.

Launched in 1999, the Euro as a cash remote places cash started out out to replace the antique currencies in member international locations. As such, the DEM (Deutsche Mark), the French Franc, and the Belgian Franc disappeared, making room for the Euro because the common overseas cash in Eurozone.

Today's Forex dashboard may be poorer in terms of the foreign money pairs which have been modified with the useful resource of the Euro appearance, but the Euro pairs more than compensate in volatility, exchange flows, and importance.

JpegThe EURUSD, as an example, is the maximum critical overseas money pair at the dashboard. It has the tightest spreads and the most essential traded volumes of all overseas money pairs. It need to come as no surprise, due to the reality the Eurozone economies are second location in terms in their period best to the us economic device.

For the retail dealer, forex pairs which incorporates EURJPY, EURGBP, EURAUD or EURCAD play a unique position due to the fact their volatility opens up loads of opportunities on the FX marketplace.

From a essential factor of view, the HICP Inflation (Harmonized Index of Consumer Prices) is the primary monetary launch in terms of its impact at the Euro pairs' volatility. Like its pals, the ECB (European Central Bank) has a mandate that specializes in inflation, and its movements are constantly aimed toward bringing it beneath but near the 2 percent target.

Messages despatched with the useful resource of the ECB have the power to transport the Euro pairs profoundly. Traders ought to watch the ECB speeches cautiously, and use Twitter economic feeds, for instance, to live up to date with the rumors surrounding ECB movements.

Inflation comes out monthly, and the center values count range extra for the ECB than the actual HICP.

Besides inflation and the ECB interest charge alternatives, speeches, and press meetings, the PMIs in Eurozone are closely watched via Forex clients. There are handiest PMI releases, and now not 3 as within the United Kingdom: offerings and production.

What's thrilling here is that the PMIs are launched for anyone u.S.A. Of america, giving a smooth photograph of which elements of the Eurozone are outperforming or underperforming.

Next in line of importance are the GDP and the unemployment fee, and the ECB considers them each while placing economic insurance.

Chapter 6: Ecb And Its Mandate

JpegAs already said, the ECB has a mandate to deliver and maintain inflation below however close to   percent. It is significantly assumed amongst economies round the world that the two percent inflation degree ensures financial prosperity and increase.

The normal ECB response to a drop in inflation is to decrease the important issue interest charge degree, or at the least to supply a dovish sign that the charges will come down in a few unspecified time within the destiny in the future. Because shopping for and promoting is a exercise of expectations, traders acquired't wait till the ECB acts, but will promote the Euro and the Euro pairs in advance.

On the possibility hand, a spike in inflation will purpose hawkishness from the ECB and shoppers will purchase the commonplace currency in the direction of one-of-a-kind foreign exchange pairs within the the Forex market dashboard.

To fulfill its mandate, the ECB objectives for rate stability. But the definition of price stability is mostly a cause of misconception for lots consumers.

It doesn't communicate to the Euro as a overseas cash preserving a set diploma. Instead, it refers back to the ability of the ECB to keep inflation at goal. That's the stableness the ECB desires to acquire.

The ECB's ruling frame, the Governing Council (GC), meets every six weeks. Up till or 3 years inside the beyond, the GC met monthly, however these days it altered its time desk, following the course set through manner of the Federal Reserve of america of Bank of Canada which additionally meets each six weeks.

Interest fee selections are brought on Thursdays, to in form in with the financial calendar and the announcements of various relevant banks. The preference is especially anticipated, because the ECB makes excellent to talk its intentions via a carefully monitored forward steering precept.

For this motive, the real desire doesn't generate an awful lot volatility on the overseas cash pairs. However, forty-5 mins after the discharge is made, the press convention is held, and highlighting any actions the ECB will take to meet its mandate and putting the course for future changes in the financial coverage.

The ECB has a difficult interest in setting the right financial insurance for the terrific economies that comprise the Eurozone. It takes guidance from the Federal Reserve inside the United States, the hassle of the subsequent economic disaster in our e-book.

Chapter 7: Federal Reserve Of The Usastructure, Mandate, Role

Since america ended the dollar's convertibility to gold (a.K.A. Losing the gold modern day) in the early Nineteen Seventies, the Federal Reserve (Fed) have turn out to be the number one vital economic organization inside the international.

Setting the hobby price stage on the federal finances rate is not an smooth project. In truth, the Fed's alternatives have an effect on no longer satisfactory the US monetary device and its residents but moreover those within the relaxation of the arena.

As the vicinity's reserve overseas coins, the USD is the foreign coins applied in maximum international alternate. Furthermore, international loans are denominated in American greenbacks, and commodities together with oil have their charges set in USD.

It technique that every Fed desire that makes the greenback each much less luxurious or greater luxurious may also have right away repercussions all over the global. For example, rising markets are regarded for his or her huge borrowing of US bucks while the Fed slashed prices to almost zero following the 2008 economic catastrophe.

Now that the Fed has reversed the route and began to hike the federal charge variety rate over again, rising markets are finding it hard to pay off their loans because of the reality bucks are greater highly-priced. It should be smooth that a preference in a distinct part of the area is sufficient to influence economic coverage, authorities movements, and population fitness in exceptional international locations and for the duration of continents .

The real call of america crucial financial institution is the Federal Reserve System and it has twelve Federal Reserve Banks unfold anywhere inside the United States:

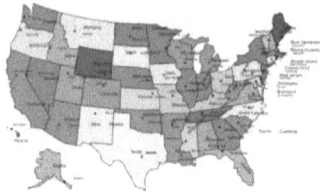

1.Boston

2.New York

three. Philadelphia

four. Cleveland

five. Richmond

6. Atlanta

7.Chicago

8. St. Luis

9. Minneapolis

10. Kansas City

eleven. Dallas

12.San Francisco

The ruling body is known as the Board of Governors. Located in Washington, D.C., it has seven members nominated via the USA President and authorized with the resource of the Senate.

Despite many human beings wondering that the Board of Governors gadgets the Fed's economic insurance, the reality is distinct. All Board individuals are a part of the FOMC (Federal Open Market Committee), the body that sincerely gadgets the economic coverage.

The FOMC releases a declaration at the federal fee range charge every six weeks, on a Wednesday. Every 2d assembly, the announcement is found up thru a press conference, in which press representatives ask questions concerning the modern-day and destiny economic coverage changes.

In modern years, the Fed has never changed the federal rate range diploma at a assembly that wasn't located with the useful resource of way of a press conference. For this motive, the volatility surrounding conferences with a scheduled press convention to conform with is better than in any other case.

For all of the motives defined on this ebook and the others of our series, that is the most essential market event for foreign cash investors. But the stock and bond markets, in addition to everyday options and futures markets, all tremble whilst the Fed makes a selection whether or now not to modify the hobby fee at the arena's reserve foreign exchange.

But what makes the Fed exchange the financial coverage? To start with, it has one of the maximum complex mandates inside the worldwide of widespread banks, a twin one. Not excellent does the Fed need to manipulate inflation, but it furthermore has to create jobs.

Chapter 8: What Matters For The Aussie Dollar

The Australian Dollar (AUD) is a darling for forex investors round the world. It has had a superb interest charge for a long time, a file superior to many different loose-floating currencies.

That method that the AUD pairs have a exceptional transfer, and this attracts shoppers on the long side. You need to understand by way of way of the usage of now what a nice trade is; we dealt with the idea in preceding books. As a reminder: it's far the interest rate differential a few of the 2 currencies that make up a pair, and can be amazing or terrible.

Charged on the prevent of the shopping for and selling day, it diminishes or will increase the equity within the buying and selling account. Obviously, for switch-paying debts, the proper trade may want to have a incredible trade.

Also referred to as the Aussie greenback, the AUD is an vital foreign coins inside the Asian part of the arena. Since 1959, the Reserve Bank of Australia (RBA) has set the financial policy for the Australian Dollar, recognized formerly as the Australian Pound, due to the u . S .'s ties with the previous British Empire.

Naturally, the interest fee choices are those who set the tone for the AUD shoppers. In sharp evaluation with the Fed and the ECB, the RBA makes a choice on the hobby rate monthly, on the begin of the month, continuously on a Tuesday.

It makes the AUD incredibly volatile, specifically if the selection comes inside the NFP week. That shape of week is hard to trade due to the truth the RBA is due on

Tuesday, the ADP inside the United States on Wednesday and the NFP on Friday. As a give up give up end result, many customers choose to attend till the NFP until deciding on an actual feature.

In the overdue 1990s the RBA delivered its inflation-targeted mandate, just like the rest of the vital banks inside the global. Targeting percent seems logical, especially if one considers the duration of high inflation in Australia at a few stage in the overdue '60s and early '70s, with levels near to twenty% ingesting away at human beings's monetary monetary financial savings.

Currency consumers interested in the AUD pairs take a look at the CPI (Consumer Price Index) as an indication of what the RBA will do next. Sometimes, the RBA Governor explicitly intervenes inside the market, as changed into the case with the preceding Governor, Stevens. In an interview with a financial e-book, he in particular asserted that the honest fee for the Australian Dollar in opposition to its U.S. Counterpart must be somewhere round zero.70.

At that factor, the AUDUSD pair become trading well above the zero.Ninety mark, and customers have been taken aback to pay interest what the RBA discovered due to the fact the trustworthy price. Needless to mention, the pair dropped in a ordinary bearish trend till the apparently desired RBA diploma became reached.

Besides the CPI, no awesome traditional economic facts is that relevant for Aussie customers. Yes, the GDP offers a glimpse into the Australian financial machine's standard ordinary performance, but it not often movements the market.

Instead, Aussie buyers need to be aware of numerous topics at the equal time as looking for or selling the Australian Dollar. Commodity expenses and the dominion of the Chinese economic gadget, to cite examples, depend greater for the AUD's volatility.

Australia has big natural property, being a internet exporter of commodities round the sector. It has one in every of the most important mining industries within the global, and its GDP relies upon cautiously at the

mining region exports.

For this motive, it employs severa human beings in the mining corporation, every upstream and downstream, in addition to in associated organizations, making it a vital region for the Australian monetary gadget.

And bet which u . S . Is the largest importer of Australian devices? That's proper, China!

That manner that AUD customers want to have an eye fixed on Chinese economic growth. If the Chinese economic system is prepared to stall or fall into recession, demand for Australian gadgets will fall, and the primary market to react is the forex market, thru way of selling the Australian Dollar.

On the opportunity hand, if the Chinese financial system is in appropriate shape, the path of least resistance is that imports will stay at the least at the equal stage, if no longer developing, and that is remarkable for the Australian Dollar.

The hassle is that the Chinese facts isn't honest. Traders must apprehend that the Chinese economic device is carefully held, and facts isn't always as obvious or broadly to be had as in capitalistic global locations. For this motive, you could in no manner be pretty fantastic whether or not or now not or not the facts release from China is reliable or no longer.

Moreover, the maximum important Chinese monetary statistics comes out on Sunday, even as the currency marketplace is closed. It reasons the Australian Dollar pairs to hole at Monday's setting out if the Chinese facts

surprises in both direction.

As for commodity charges, gold is a superb benchmark for the AUDUSD pair. For years, the correlation most of the two economic merchandise became so close to that each one you had to do to change the AUDUSD pair end up to check at wherein the price of gold became going.

In sum, besides the usual financial releases used to interpret an financial system, the Forex market clients have to have an eye constant at the Chinese monetary gadget and the charge evolution on the commodity markets, specially gold and unique precious metals.

Chapter 9: Bank Of Canada And The Loonie Dollar

The Loonie is the nickname for the Canadian Dollar (CAD). It is a curious forex, to mention the least, with the most unpredictable behavior possible to look inside the distant places money marketplace.

It can be due to the fact the Canadian economic gadget in all fairness uncommon. With large natural resources and a heavy dependence on the fee of oil, Canada built its financial system at the energy business enterprise.

Oil is, in all likelihood, the most important commodity of our time. We don't recognize what the future may also additionally supply, however looking lower again in time we can say that the ultimate centuries' technological advances are due to the invention of oil.

Almost the whole thing we do these days has a strong reference to oil. For this motive, oil-rich countries loved excellent fortunes and changed their financial device dramatically (e.G. Saudi Arabia).

In the case of Canada, oil plays a important feature. And because it stocks a border with the largest monetary tool in the world (United States), over seventy five% of Canadian oil exports go to america.

For this reason, the oil inventories within the United States is one of the maximum essential quantities of facts that impacts the fee of the Canadian Dollar. Everyone keeps a watch constant on the oil consumption within the most critical financial system within the global, from buyers to the Bank of Canada and the Fed.

The Canadian Dollar, therefore, enjoys an immediate correlation with the rate of oil, due to the truth the Canadian monetary gadget is so power-based one. The arithmetic is straightforward: lower oil price outcomes in a lower GDP, as a stop end result bad for the foreign exchange, on the same time as better oil prices are a internet awesome for the Canadian Dollar.

Along the equal line, OPEC (Organization of Petroleum Exporting Countries) conferences and production choices that affect the steadiness of deliver and demand are also key while buying and selling the CAD pairs. Put truly, any oil-associated information or event impacts the fee of the Loonie dollar even greater than BOC's (Bank of Canada) movements can also.

And now you apprehend why the Bank of Canada and its hobby charge selections aren't in first region close to influencing the CAD's price. In fact, no longer as quickly as has the marketplace reversed a Bank of Canada's desire on a few oil-related facts.

It is properly clearly really worth bringing up that Bank of Canada meets each six weeks to set the hobby charge stage for the CAD. BOC broadcasts the destiny economic policy continuously on a Wednesday and it's far one of the critical banks that likes to take markets with the useful aid of marvel.

Chapter 10: Interpreting The Housing Data In The United States

After the 2008 financial disaster, no person harbors any doubts about the housing area's importance. It is a unique location that tells lots approximately what's taking area in an financial system.

For instance, it's far a pronouncing that virtually by means of using counting the style of cranes in a rustic you'll understand if the financial system is increasing or contracting. A supplier that uses important evaluation to interpret economies and speculate on their currencies will find out such information very beneficial.

The United States is the handiest main monetary gadget that presents housing statistics as a awesome piece of economic releases. In each other a part of the world, the regular launch is the PMI Construction, as in the United Kingdom, for example.

Any PMI is interpreted based at the 50 level, with better values suggesting 1 / 4 that is increasing, and decrease ones a place that is contracting. Obviously, the PMI record is extra than definitely the launched fee.

It is an entire assessment of the whole manufacturing and housing zone. However, few investors in reality open the record and try to understand the overall photo. Which, of course, is to the detriment of a accurate evaluation.

This is why the united states housing statistics deserves unique interest. First, it's miles to be had in distinct releases, throughout the searching for and selling month. Second, the desired opinions inform the real kingdom of the vicinity, starting with the constructing permits issued and completing with the homes supplied or that remained in inventory.

In a shopping for and selling month, the number one piece of statistics approximately the housing region comes out seventeen days after the start of the month. On the 18th of each month, Building Permits well-knownshows the annualized range of allows issued.

The hobby right right right here is at the word "annualized." It way that the format is the monthly determine times three hundred and sixty five days which is probably in a twelve months. It tasks destiny production interest in the United States because of the reality obtaining a constructing allow is the primary element that has to take vicinity on the equal time as constructing a new building. Naturally, the larger the quantity, the more exquisite for the USD.

Together with the Building Permits launch, the Housing Starts show the residential houses that began manufacturing within the preceding month. The launch is carefully correlated with the Building Permits, and buyers search for a discrepancy the various 2. Any anomaly is interpreted as a miscalculation and an opportunity to shop for or promote the USD.

Existing Home Sales show the kind of devices supplied in the course of the previous month and versions on this range create masses of volatility on the foreign exchange market.

Almost thirty days after the month ends, the Pending Home Sales launch suggests the ability housing on sale pipeline and is a super indication of the health of the housing area.

All the releases collectively provide traders the chance to shape a solid image of one of the maximum dynamic sectors of america monetary tool.

Chapter 11: Bank Of England And Its Role At The Pound's Fluctuation

Bank of England (BOE) is one of the oldest essential banks within the worldwide. It dictates the monetary coverage on the British Pound (GBP), a liquid and very volatile free-floating forex.

On these days's the Forex market dashboard, the pound is the choice of purchasers looking for foreign money pairs that excursion more than the commonplace ATR. It is known that the GBP pairs like GBPUSD, GBPCHF or GBPJPY have wider every day ranges than, say EURUSD or USDCAD.

BOE has an inflationary mandate. We already defined on this ebook how the Inflation Letter works and what the BOE does whilst inflation deviates multiple percentage from the purpose. The purpose, as we've stated, is percentage, and is stylish at some point of all capitalistic global places.

Bank of England's ruling body is called the MPC (Monetary Policy Committee) and it releases the hobby charge desire each six weeks, on a Thursday. It was as soon as a month-to-month assembly, but BOE accompanied the course set with the useful resource of the Fed and modified the time table.

One element to recognize even as shopping for and selling BOE interest rate picks is that there can be no press convention to examine the MPC announcement if the interest price remains unchanged. In unique phrases, all you get is the assertion that the BOE left the interest expenses unchanged and that's it.

Obviously, the pound doesn't do masses in such instances, and the BOE turns its hobby to the Inflation Letter and uses that press convention to speak to markets its intentions.

For a number one economic organization that has stood the check of time, Bank of England transformed itself proper into a modern-day corporation focused now on proscribing the liabilities of the Brexit choice. Setting the financial coverage in the kind of difficult surroundings proves to be a hard mission, specially considering the GBP's volatility.

Chapter 12: News Trading Vs. Technical Trading

The foreign exchange marketplace is so large that the dimensions of retail trading is insignificant. Only approximately five or six percentage of the market belongs to stores, with the relaxation to institutional buyers, agents, industrial and big banks, and so forth.

Yet, each market participant, no matter its period and assets, faces the equal choice: to alternate information or occasions that skip the marketplace or to use technical setups. Or both.

Naturally, the identical antique answer is that shoppers need to apply each information and technical looking for and promoting. But this is more tough to do than many investors like to admit.

There's a predilection for both technical or critical analysis. In the surrender, consumers use them each, but opportunities differ.

For example, a information provider will continuously emphasize the vital facet of a change extra than the technical one. He/she is aware about the basics of technical analysis, but the middle of their trading alternatives is essential.

The different manner round works as nicely. Technical customers do remember information releases as functionality motives for market actions, but for them the choice to shop for or sell a overseas coins pair comes from subjects which include manual and resistance, trendlines, buying and selling theories, and so forth.

Therefore, there's a natural break up at the same time as shopping for and promoting the foreign exchange market and buyers pick each vital or technical evaluation to popularity on. For maximum retail customers, essential assessment way facts buying and selling.

News trading has every advantages and downsides. It is a notable way to make a brief dollar, and that is why it attracts such numerous retail traders as absolutely everyone desires to turn a small account into a bigger one as brief as viable.

However, records purchasing for and selling is ruled via the use of algorithms, robots that purchase and promote the market automatically. These machines are programmed by using way of quant organizations and can execute plenty of trades in step with 2nd, on foot state-of-the-art math computations while trading.

Ever questioned why the market explodes higher or sinks lower in a break up-2nd at the equal time as a few crucial records hits the wires? It's because of the buying and selling algorithms that buy or promote on the equal

time.

It is said that they're "glued" to the wires, in the texture that orders already exist to buy or promote a forex pair if/while some thing specific takes vicinity. The monetary calendar that we explained in one of the previous chapters of this ebook is a super manner to understand statistics buying and selling.

Traders understand in advance what the essential occasions in the week in advance might be. Also, the preceding and the forecast price are there.

These machines or buying and promoting algorithms are recommended to shop for or promote based on what the actual will show. They'll act in the blink of an eye fixed, and ship the market better or lower without word.

A sharp bypass like that is each a blessing and a curse. If you're on the right component of the market, profits are made right now. But if not, the cash from the looking for and promoting account in truth vanishes.

When the usage of information trading, the easy principle is to in no way gamble on a facts launch. Savvy shoppers look ahead to the primary marketplace reaction in advance than coming into the marketplace.

They live up for the records to come out and for the algorithms to make the first flow. Then, traders pass at the decrease timeframes together with the 5-minute or perhaps the most effective-minute chart and exchange inside the equal path due to the reality the preliminary market response when the marketplace reaches overbought or oversold tiers.

Therefore, the smart technique for facts shopping for and selling is a aggregate some of the buying and selling set of rules's response and technical evaluation.

With this bankruptcy, we tried to illustrate that there's a strong link amongst statistics shopping for and promoting and technical shopping for and promoting and traders do use them every, irrespective of generally relying extra on one over the other.

Fundamental buyers, therefore, do use technical evaluation to verify their thesis, at the identical time as technical consumers do use information shopping for and promoting due to the fact the purpose why the market travels.

Chapter 13: Macroeconomicshow Investing Starts

Time is the best element that differentiates buying and selling strategies. Different buying and promoting patterns are primarily based at the time-horizon of a alternate.

Scalping is buying and selling with a short or very short-time period time horizon, and traders use decrease timeframes along side the 5-minute or perhaps the one-minute chart. Swing shopping for and selling is at the equal time as customers are inclined to keep positions open a number of hours and as a good deal as multiple weeks and now and again extra.

A supplier is Investing at the same time as time isn't always an problem. It doesn't rely WHEN the market turns or reaches the reason, it is greater a depend of being right or incorrect.

Investors have a look at the identical monetary data as traders using news buying and promoting, however they don't trade in the market skip generated with the useful resource of the records. Instead, purchasers use the monetary statistics and put together a evaluation of an financial system.

Typically, traders are early in a alternate, due to the truth they constantly try to count on the following market cycle. Macroeconomic evaluation is the gadget of searching at severa economies in awesome part of the arena and making an investment based at the final outcomes.

It is a complicated analytical gadget that calls for masses of capital and staying electricity. Macro-traders buy or promote a forex pair based totally absolutely totally on versions in economic pointers. If the market doesn't quick react find it irresistible is supposed to do, that's now not a trouble.

The famous investor Carl Icahn stated that he shorted the EURUSD a few years inside the past at around 1.27 in the returned of the Eurozone troubles, the ECB easing and the

Fed not inclined to transport the federal budget rate beneath 0.

The macro-assessment proved to be right, because the EURUSD pair collapsed to nearly parity. However, in advance than collapsing, it moved first to at the least one.Forty three, pretty a distance. Many retail customers can't provide you with the cash for this form of a headwind, however investors, yet again, have every the persistence and capital to stand as much as such marketplace conditions.

Value-investing is a similar approach to shopping for and selling using macro-analysis, the difference being exquisite that buyers the usage of rate-making an funding are energetic on the inventory market, now not the foreign exchange marketplace.

Chapter 14: Explaining Forward Guidance

Forward steerage have become a de-facto economic coverage device simplest these days. Up until the 2008 monetary catastrophe, all critical banks needed to do end up to decrease the interest charge level at the same time as inflation dropped, or hike it while inflation moved to the upside.

The manner, called monetary easing in the first case and financial tightening in the 2d one, modified into honest and there were fewer surprises down the street. However, as soon as the 2008 monetary disaster ignited within the United States, it have come to be crystal easy that this modified into a worldwide catastrophe and no longer a close-by one.

The manner the financial device capabilities in the 21st century doesn't allow a trouble to live close by, due to the fact the complete global had publicity at the U.S. Housing market and at the U.S. Dollar.

When the Fed decreased the costs to zero in an in a unmarried day skip, it eased conditions on the most important financial machine inside the international and effectively supplied liquidity to enterprise banks beneath stress. The concept have become to stimulate enterprise banks to take extra risks and make investments inside the financial device.

It didn't paintings, because banks have been greater worried about liquidity and capital and had been the use of their extra reserves, if any, to cover for his or her NPLs (Non-Performing Loans). But as it grew to become out, the Fed modified into quite an present day organization.

Under the close to steerage of Ben Bernanke, it started out out looking for U.S. Government bonds in a way dubbed Quantitative Easing (QE). But that changed into handiest one of the exceptional and unconventional measures keen on the aid of using the Fed.

The Fed come to be the primary to understand the antique way of sporting out financial insurance have come to be over. The worldwide changed, economies changed, and monetary coverage had to do the identical.

One of the cleverest thoughts the Fed had changed into to create a brand new gadget to speak to markets. Because buying and selling economic markets is governed with the useful useful resource of algorithmic operations, markets can disintegrate proper away if the communication tool isn't finished carefully.

So the Fed initiated a in advance steering precept, fast located via the use of one in all a kind primary banks within the worldwide, inclusive of the ECB. The idea is quite easy: to higher speak to markets what the intentions are for the destiny and higher give an cause of monetary insurance decisions.

Moreover, under the ahead steerage principle, important banks moreover installation specific conditions wanted for the vital financial group to do so. For example, within the path of the QE packages, the Fed used the Unemployment Rate degree to sign the stop of the applications.

In one in all a type terms, the very last round of QE come to be alleged to final handiest until the Unemployment Rate reached a exceptional degree. Everyone concerned in buying and selling the foreign places coins marketplace knew that, so even as the Unemployment Rate have been given close to the purpose, the USD rose because of the truth the easing method have grow to be supposed to forestall.

Chapter 15: Deflation Vs. Inflationhow To Fight Them

Throughout this e-book and the alternative ones of our collection, you've heard many things approximately inflation. It plays a essential role in buying and selling the foreign cash marketplace because of the truth important banks run their financial insurance based totally on the level of inflation.

Most foremost banks recall the 2 percentage aim to be wholesome for steady financial increase, however that would alternate within the future. For now, it stays the road in the sand for applicable banking around the sector.

Inflation refers to a upward push inside the rate of products and services. It stimulates consumption, and intake is the exceptional aspect that makes an economic gadget expand.

Here's an example. Assume you need to shop for something, permit's say a laptop.

If the price of the computer rises, even a bit, in a brief length, you'll be tempted to shop for it faster out of worry of getting to pay more for it in the future. In tremendous phrases, you're now not postponing the buying preference, and the object had been given offered.

The supplier will region an order to the manufacturer, the manufacturer will start building materials to fabricate it, humans may want to have solid jobs, and the authorities has much less unemployment benefits to pay. Not to say people are happier due to the truth a developing economic system brings excessive ranges of personal delight.

So that's the motive why inflation subjects for vital banking. When it rises over the 2 percentage aim, the essential monetary organization will become alarmed. There's too much coins inside the economic system, and the monetary enterprise will start a "draining" system, through the usage of raising the interest charges.

By doing that, it stimulates industrial banks to prevent lending to organizations and the general populace, and in reality positioned their greater reserves in in a single day deposits with the fundamental monetary institution. For that, they'll get preserve of confident interest, without taking the vain dangers associated with lending.

The better inflation is going, the higher the hobby fees will go. But, as we'll show in the subsequent bankruptcy, that's not constantly the notable answer, as hyperinflation is a real hazard.

The example with the laptop used proper here shows why a certain inflation stage allows an monetary system. But what do you do whilst the fee of a terrific or company falls?

Clearly, the number one reaction of maximum human beings is that it's now a good deal and that's splendid for a deal. It can be so, however that's most effective on first appearance, and it's a situation you don't need to have for an prolonged term.

If charges keep falling, humans will preserve postponing their purchasing choicesout of fear of lacking out on an terrific decrease fee inside the future. Retailers won't promote anymore, inventories will upward push, manufacturers will should lay off humans, unemployment will rise, and the monetary gadget will fall into recession.

When inflation falls below 0, it is stated that the economic system reached deflationary territory, and that's very hard for essential banks to fight. One easy reaction is to cut interest expenses, however up until presently, essential banks in no manner dropped the price below zero.

Nowadays, however, horrific fees are a fact, and a few economies live resilient regardless of such stimulus. We can say, without a shadow of doubt, that amongst inflation or deflation, the second is a protracted way worse for an monetary machine and populace than the primary one is.

So, from this second on, while you see the expenses of merchandise and offerings dropping, assume instances whether or now not it's an exquisite or a awful element. Not most effective as it doesn't supply some aspect correct for the financial system, but it indicators deeper and large problems in

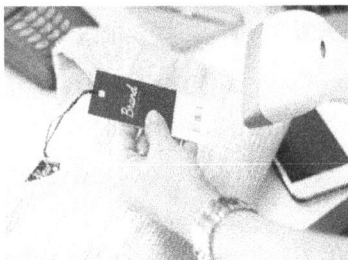

advance.

Chapter 16: Hyperinflation Or What Happens When Money Dies

As we get closer to the prevent of this ebook, we need to quit with what cash is and what it manner to humans round the arena.

Money is one of the best topics to expose as much as humankind. Because of it, we advantage from assistance inside the entirety we do in our everyday lifestyles.

Think of it! You enjoy ill? You visit the medical institution, and someone is there to cope with you. Why? Because he/she is paid to do this, and the purpose why he/she is there may be coins, not due to the reality the scientific doctor is eager on you and will in fact want to provide assist.

Or, say you need help in buying a residence, so you enlist a actual-property organization to show you round. For a fee (cash), of course..

We can find out examples, glaringly, within the entirety we do in lifestyles. Money added humans collectively, it's far the cause of unity in a society, and is a extremely good manner to accept as true with people.

Why will we communicate about cash? Well, buying and selling is all approximately money.

We, as buyers, are right right right here to make a earnings, to promote immoderate and purchase low, or to buy low and sell immoderate. If buyers do no longer understand what cash is and its importance to society, purchasing for and selling doesn't make experience.

Many human beings take coins as a proper. Money, certainly placed, is some factor one want to have.

But a near check the concept of cash and the consider that consists of it, well-knownshows a far greater state-of-the-art trouble. The recollect difficulty is what brings societies collectively, and coins is a herbal reflected picture of agree with.

What do primary banks do? They hassle portions of paper (banknotes) and unfold them round.

With that piece of paper, human beings move and buy subjects, trusting the seller can be given the paper. It is terrific how paper (inside the case of banknotes) and metal (within the case of coins) are the pillars of a device based mostly on no longer anything but trust.

I take into account you, you believe me, and anyone trusts the important financial institution. But what if the believe is broken?

When believe is long past, the coins dies. As easy as that!

When cash dies, it technique inflation is going through the roof. Unfortunately, we have examples proper inside the front of our eyes, with a few economies within the international going through horrible crises.

Venezuela, Argentina, and, to a degree, Brazil and Turkey, face tough inflationary conditions. People out of vicinity obtain as proper with in what coins is and combat hyperinflation with all way viable.

So, what's hyperinflation and why it's so essential to keep away from it? Put in reality, whilst coins isn't certainly properly really worth a few aspect, that's the forestall result of hyperinflation.

It approach that prices upward push so fast that the top notch bank can't keep tempo with interest charge hikes. Venezuela is out of this worldwide with inflation achieving 1,000,000 percent or some thing close to, and no individual trusts the Bolivar anymore.

The catastrophe despatched human beings flooding into the encircling international locations, with loads of hundreds of people moving to neighboring Brazil, Colombia, and so on. Again, don't forget became misplaced, and that's the stop of the whole thing.

The humorous issue is that the vital monetary organization can't do a whole lot about it. Look at Argentina in 2018.

Inflation runs very excessive, and the hobby fee level exceeds 45%. That's now not a typo!

While critical banks in Europe, america, Japan, United Kingdom, Australia, and so forth, set the interest rate diploma up to two percentage, in Argentina subjects went crazy. Not as crazy as in Venezuela, however close.

The idea is that cash, in the end, clearly dies while the consider inside the gadget disappears.

Why must Forex buyers care? Well, for lots motives.

First, the the Forex market provider is the primary one to realize whilst subjects circulate wrong. Because the currency market is the primary one to answer, the charge of cash adjustments first, and the people feel the very last effects later.

Second, at the same time as accept as true with is out of place, opportunities rise up. Savvy buyers do apprehend that every catastrophe has an answer, and, in the end, money received't lose its position.

However, the project is to have the capital, the right statistics, and the preference to take a wager in competition to a vicious fashion. Which, judging in competition to the whole thing we've referred to to this point, doesn't make experience.

We chose to stop this e-book with hyperinflation as everyone has to apprehend the role coins performs in our lives. And also, the tough venture essential banks have.

It isn't a thriller that many human beings hate number one banks. They think about a "device" or "cartel" that manipulates the hobby costs for private benefit.

If there's one detail to eliminate from studying this ebook, it's far the complexity of important banking and why it's miles vital for the whole lot we do in our lives. So earlier than announcing some component horrible approximately a vital financial organization to any extent in addition, suppose instances at the implications and the duty that valuable bankers have.

We save you this e-book with an picture of the world's reserve foreign exchange inside

the twenty first-century: the U.S. Dollar.

Chapter 17: Setting Up Your Equipment

One of the maximum essential things a provider dreams is a first-rate computer.

While you don't must go for super expensive ones proper out of the gate, we are able to bypass over the basics that you need for your tool: tool protection, internet connection, software application, and hardware.

Hardware

Each issuer is privy to what they'll be searching out in a device, so noclients are going to be alike. There are some fundamentals, although, that day shoppers need in a pc and its hardware:

- Windows eight.1 or better working gadget. A 64-bit OS is preferred

- eight GB of RAM, 16 GB or greater is desired

- Intel Core i5 or Intel Core i7

- Two 21-inch LCD video display gadgets. This is non-compulsory for the newbie. There's no need to strain over having a couple of video display units whilst you're virtually starting out. You can make bigger your set as you pass alongside.

Unless you're surely pinnacle with editing computer systems, and you already know what you're doing, you should purchase your computer tool with it already installation based totally definitely totally on the manner you need it.

Software

All buyers ought to have a software program platform to shop for and promote on. This may be hooked up in your laptop which you have completely for buying and selling. This is wherein a dealer will observe futures, shares, currencies, and so forth, and could region their orders. This might be the most essential trouble you may must pick out out, so you need to make certain you apprehend what you need out of your software program. If you are making plans on trading shares, you must look for a platform that has:

• Order get entry to built into the software program program

• Real-time information

• Portfolio tracker

• Real-time streaming charts and prices that continuously replace

• Sales and time lists of all transactions

• Level II

Internet connection

If you don't have a splendid net connection, you obtained't be capable of exchange. Here are some ideal net connections to choose out from:

● Cable modem service

This is the popular preference. The speeds of cable internet can range from five Mbps to 100 Mbps counting on the issuer provider.

● Digital Subscriber Line (DSL)

You can discover DSL speeds from one Mbps to eight Mbps. DSL is also sensitive to distance, so relying on how a protracted way away your buying and selling computer is to the number one hub or workplace that gives your service, the slower it's far going to be.

● Fiber-Optic Internet Service

This is a genuinely perfect alternative. FTTH is the gold widespread net, but it's not available in very many locations. Residential clients are drooling for fiber net. A suitable example is probably Google Fiber, that might provide you with speeds of a thousand Mbps. If you've got get right of entry to to fiber net in your location, then you truely definately need to have it to trade.

System safety

No depend what you do on the computer, whether or now not it's buying and selling or socializing, you're nevertheless at threat for viruses. That's why you need to make sure that you protect your laptop from the worst. There arestyles of protection you could depend on:

● Antivirus

Viruses can reason important, irreparable damage in your laptop. Many pc structures already have antivirus software software established on it, but it generally slows your laptop down. Make fine you do a piece of research in advance than you choose your antivirus software program software.

● Firewall

If you operate a connection like cable net or DSL, then you definately definately are at a better chance of malware or hacking. Getting firewall safety also can require more software software or hardware which you need to put in on your pc. A software software program firewall is the proper possibility. Again, do loads of studies earlier than creating a buy.

Now that you understand what you want, it's time to get topics installation.

Chapter 18: Learn The Important Rules

All of those hints and facts approximately day looking for and selling need to be observed out and memorized due to the reality they need to be accompanied continuously.

These are all commonplace revel in regulations, as nicely. One of the most important motives why humans become losing coins is because they don't have a simple records of those important necessities. Some of those can also seem simplistic, however they are crucial:

• To alternate shares, by means of way of the usage of law in the US, you want to have $25,000 or extra. To day exchange currencies, you most effective want to have a few hundred.

• What day buying and selling in reality is, due to the fact the time period 'day buying and selling' is every so often misused, real day trading approach that you don't preserve a position in a unmarried day. You remove it on the equal day to procure it. If you exchange currencies, there's no such element as an in a single day characteristic due to the fact trade in the markets stays on for twenty-4/7.

● You should ensure that your losses are limited whilst shopping for and selling. This is probably the maximum essential rule and one as a manner to be advanced on in a later step.

● Trading want to best be finished with a part of your cash. This manner that you want to fine use a number of your coins to day trade. This is because of the reality you in no way understand if you are going to obtain achievement. Make nice you can give you the money for to change with the coins you operate.

● You need to have right exercise and education. This is just like any other commercial enterprise enterprise business enterprise. You want to make certain you realize what you are doing.

- The time it'll take you to have a look at trading will range from character to man or woman.

- You want a proper away-get proper of access to provider so that you can start day buying and promoting shares.

- Setting every day cash desires aren't going to help you as an afternoon dealer.

- There is not any rule that asserts you need to trade each single day. On a few days, there may not be any pinnacle trades to make. On in recent times, you have to have a have a look at, observe, and workout. Don't just make a change because of the reality you consider you studied you want to.

Make Sure You Understand the Basics

To be a day dealer, it would assist in case you understood some of the fundamentals about making an investment. It's moreover crucial which you recognise what 'bid and ask' is, and the awesome order kinds that you could area even as you purchase and sell. We'll in quick pass over some of the ones, however you continue to want to take more time on day 3 to study extra about this stuff.

Bid and Ask

If you had been to visit a monetary net site and kind within the ticker photo for a stock, you may get plenty of numbers after phrases like EPS, marketplace cap, div & yield, quantity, beta, P/E, fiftywk variety, day's variety, open, previous near. This is known as diploma I data. This data offers you the satisfactory to be had price for a inventory at a superb time.

If we checked out Intel (INTC) Corporation's stock information, we'd see:

● EPS – 2.30

This suggests how worthwhile a business corporation enterprise is.

● Market cap – 273.41B

This is the marketplace fee of the organization.

- Div & Yield – 1.20/2.10%

This is the proportion of dividends a company can pay out each year.

- Volume – 31,183,166.00

This is the whole quantity of stocks that have been offered and provided.

- Beta – 1.207

This shows the volatility. Over one approach it's more risky than the marketplace.

- P/E – 24.Eighty

This is the fee-to-profits ratio discovered thru dividing the marketplace charge and EPS.

- fiftyWk Range – 33.23-57.10

This is the very great and lowest rate that a stock has been over the past three hundred and sixty five days.

- Days Range – fifty five.Eighty-fifty seven.10

This is the extremely good and lowest fee that a inventory has reached in the last looking for and selling day.

- Open – fifty five.Eighty four

This is the last charge the stock opened at.

- Prev Close – fifty 5.20

This is the ultimate price the stock closed at.

These are the numbers you'll be looking at at the same time as you're deciding on a stock.

Types of orders

Market order

This is an order to sell or buy a inventory on the fantastic bid or to invite whilst an order receives to marketplace. A lot of humans will select this order due to the reality they assume it is going to be finished the fastest. This isn't the reality. This also can assure you an execution, but it may end up getting you in or out of inventory purchasing for and promoting faster than each person else. Avoid this as a bargain as you can.

Limit order

This is an order purchase or sell at a pleasant price or a better price. This want to be the order that you use the most usually. Unfortunately, this one doesn't get used as an lousy lot as it must because human beings are afraid their order acquired't be executed.

Stop order

This is an order that becomes a market order as soon as a effective charge is hit. This is regularly used to restriction losses or to shield a dealer's earnings.

Chapter 19: Open Your Brokerage Account

When it entails beginning your brokerage account, you want to test some things like margin quotes, commissions, and awesome prices. You also can want to conquer the marketplace change after alternate, however if you don't select an notable dealer, it can end up costing you all your winnings.

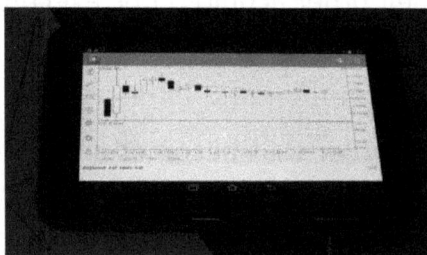

For a excessive-quantity dealer, they will emerge as paying out commission costs up into the hundreds or hundreds every unmarried day. If a dealer is aware about that they may exchange on a immoderate quantity, they need to contact a broker and take a look at out their net internet site to appearance what their expenses are.

Once you take a look at out the brokerage's charge and costs, you want to take a look at the platform they've got. The platform could have an effect on such things as execution tempo and rate charges. As an afternoon dealer, you don't need to end up experiencing a expensive -2nd put off in a few unspecified time inside the future of processing. A lot of dealers have actual-time executions, however slippage can despite the fact that display up. You want to try out a brokerage's platform to peer if you need the way it sincerely works.

You should additionally have a look at their customer service and economic stability. Customer company is crucial because of the fact you want a brokerage that let you speedy in case of a catastrophe, like a computer crash or a few unique form of failure. This will assist if you need to get out of a trade short and a trouble takes location collectively with your device. Financial power is crucial because of the reality dealers can, and have, lengthy long past out of organization. This can grow to be costing your entire account.

Some brokerages to check out are:

- Interactive agents

- TradeStation

- Lightspeed

- TD Ameritrade

- Fidelity

- E-Trade

- OptionsXpress

- SpeedTrader

- Generic Trade

- MB Trading

Day five:

Create a Solid Trading Foundation

Creating a buying and promoting basis is greater of a intellectual guidance inside the path of purchasing and selling than a bodily one. Here, you may ensure which you are doing this for the right reasons.

First, you want to determine out why you need to change. There may be a whole lot of motives for someone to start buying and promoting, and there's no such element as a wrong solution. The first-rate incorrect solution is when you have no reason, or you say some issue along the strains of: "I concept I'd deliver it a attempt." You need to have a awesome cause, a sturdy motivation. Otherwise, you received't acquire fulfillment.

Next, you want to recognize that an amazing manner to make cash as a issuer you have to discover ways to now not lose cash. How is this done? By 'now not losing the wooded area some of the wooden.'

You want to just accept the truth that traders make their coins from the threshold of their looking for and promoting tool, which their method gives them over time. It doesn't come from an individual trade or a series of trades. In order to just accept this, you want to discover ways to take possession of your technique. If you skip this, you'll be taking a soar of faith. You pleasant think that your method is going to work and not surely believing it will.

Lastly, you want to keep it clean. You want to realise whilst to save you, and you have to virtually have a strict schedule each day. A lot of humans say which you need to simplest alternate between the hole of the USA session and noon. This will exchange counting on what markets and time zones you advise on shopping for and selling in.

Set Up Your Mindset

Again, this step is all about your attitude. Your thoughts and feelings play a huge detail in day buying and selling, and it's critical that you acquire the stuff you cannot change.

Pick out a newbie's marketplace

This is a marketplace in which you can chance handiest two percentage or less with an account of most effective $5,000. A outstanding start may additionally the NASDAQ E-mini a hundred and forty four tick chart. Here you could change one settlement, and your chance is generally underneathpercent.

Manually backtest

You ought to ensure which you recognize the way to backtest your technique. I realise you haven't decided the way to make a method however, but you want to get your mind organized for what's to return returned. Don't take everybody else's word for it, as you've got to check a approach yourself.

Witness your backtest end result

Take word of the losses as they have a examine for your winners. You can't allow your emotions get the extraordinary of you really due to the truth you had severa consecutive losses. Your income will, or did pick out another time up. It doesn't depend what number of losses you are taking in a row, what topics is which you located out it, adjusted topics, after which made up for it. This is wherein your thoughts-set comes into play. You have to take ownership of your gadget.

Be like a agency

Rome wasn't constructed in an afternoon. You can't simply shorten the ones steps. You must take internal ownership of all of this. Shortcuts will end up costing you cash. Successful day buying and promoting isn't a magical region that makes you cash. It works much like a business company.

Create a Risk Management Plan

Risk manage is a vital, but regularly omitted, a part of a a achievement trader. In all honesty, a supplier that has made pretty a piece of earnings over their time as a dealer can lose it all in more than one horrible trades within the event that they don't have an terrific chance control plan. This chapter is going to transport over some easy strategies that you could protect all of your searching for and promoting earnings. While ninety% of a supplier's trades might be winning, if 10% of the change losses are mishandled, they will lose coins on a day by day foundation.

For an afternoon company, danger manipulate is one of the maximum important topics, subsequent to springing up with a buying and promoting approach. Even the maximum experienced day supplier can't say they'll be excellent, and they all will make losing trades. Having a properly-greased threat manipulate technique is what offers a provider the hazard to lose on trades with out experiencing any irreparable harm to their searching for and promoting money owed.

Chapter 20: Stop-Loss And Take-Earnings

Take-income and stop-loss factors arevital techniques in which a supplier can plan out their trades. A pinnacle provider is privy to what rate they might pay and the charge that they need to promote for. They then compare the returns they get within the direction of the chances of their stock hitting its purpose. If they get an adjusted return that is large sufficient, they may choose to make the exchange.

On the flip aspect, the unsuccessful dealer will skip right into a alternate without understanding any elements wherein they should sell at a loss or earnings. This is similar to gamblers which may be on an unlucky or lucky streak, the feelings will start to control them and could start dictating their trades. Losses generally have a tendency to provoke people to preserve a inventory and desire that they will get their cash over again. Profits commonly will be inclined to entice the provider to hold inside the hopes of creating even extra cash.

Stop-loss points are the rate in which a dealer goes to sell stock and take a loss. This will frequently stand up whilst a exchange starts offevolved to move in an sudden, awful course. These factors are created to keep the company from questioning they will get their cash another time and restriction their losses before they get too top notch. For instance, if a inventory goes under a super help degree, then a supplier will sell rapid.

A take-earnings is a place where a issuer will promote their stock and take a profits on their alternate. This is normally in which a further upside is limited given the viable risks. An example of this may be the stock getting close to an critical resistance degree after it had commenced making a big upward flow. The supplier must need to put off it earlier than a consolidation period takes place.

Understand the Markets

If you really want to make cash in a totally aggressive and quite atypical device, then it's vital that you apprehend those 5 things about the marketplace:

The Stock Market

The stock market is a totally complicated device wherein human beings buy and sell shares of agencies.

The Adversarial Trading System

The stock marketplace brings in a set of hundreds and masses of consumers with quite unique views. The motive for that is because at the same time as one individual sells a stock, there should be anybody else so as to buy it. Since both of them can't be proper, that makes it an hostile gadget. Basically, one individual will gain from every one of a kind person's struggling.

Prices cross up and down

A lot of various things will have an effect on the expenses inside the market. Things like an abundance of or loss of appropriate alternatives, supply and phone for, social and political unrest, natural disasters, evaluations of well-known customers, and the media may additionally have an effect at the fee.

Difficult to are searching forward to

Investors can't anticipate precisely what the stock market goes to do. They can use figures and evaluation to bet or estimate what it will do, but they won't ever understand precisely. Things like stock valuation, human choice approach, and a triggering occasion are all that makes the stock marketplace unpredictable.

When to buy and sell

The two biggest alternatives for a provider are when to shop for and while to promote. Buying is tremendous carried out while different buyers and traders are pessimistic. Selling is first-rate executed whilst specific traders and traders are wonderful. But caution should typically be exercised

Picking Stocks to Trade

You ought to choose out your shares primarily based on quite a number of things, which embody your enjoy diploma, the capital you've got, and your fashion of buying and selling. You need to make certain that you write down your necessities in your shares and hold that as part of your searching for and selling plan. Your looking for and selling plan, which we are capable of get to in a later financial ruin, will constantly evolve as you boom as a trader.

You have to have get right of entry to to gear like stage II, beta, and stage I that will help you make your selections higher. It moreover permits to determine out the diploma of threat that you are adequate residing with. You need to provide you a inventory deciding on approach if you need to preserve your capital and decrease the dangers.

There is a huge style of stocks that you can alternate, and they'll include one-of-a-type quantity, volatility, and charge traits. Your first step is to make sure you lessen your hazard. As you start to evolve, and you have a set up success charge, now you could boom your stock choosing approach.

No count the technique you come up with, you want to stick with fine searching for and promoting one stock at a time, initially. Even a number of the most a achievement traders best trade a single inventory at a time.

You must really check your shares. Every stock has their very very own behavior that you have to investigate. Study their charts at diverse excellent times. Over time, you may begin to add greater stocks on your listing.

While you are searching for and selling one stock, you have to be analyzing others to feature on your listing. The critical issue is to ensure that your shares align collectively along with your buying and selling plan. Here is an example of a stock deciding on approach:

- I first-rate have 5 shares to change, and I will exceptional alternate considered one of them at a time until I'm cushty

- The charge is amongst $20 and $40

- Their common 30-day quantity is amongst one andmillion

- They have a medium diploma of volatility

- I will live away from biotech shares

- My 5 stocks may be studied each night time time time and at extraordinary timeframes

- I may additionally have a examine S&P Futures

Chapter 21: Study Your Stocks

Now that you have a manner for choosing your shares, you want to have a examine the ones stocks. Here are 10 topics which you need to take a look at whilst you're reading your stocks. These elements may additionally assist you choose out the super shares to trade:

Revenue

A inventory's increase starts offevolved offevolved with the agency being worthwhile. Revenue will provide an idea of the quantity of coins a enterprise is making. If income goes up constantly, then the industrial enterprise enterprise is developing.

● Pass: If the income goes up, then the inventory passes.

● Fail: If the sales is lowering, then the stock fails.

Earnings in line with Share

EPS suggests how a high-quality deal of the revenue is flowing into the company's stockholders. EPS is the quantity of coins the business business enterprise makes in income in step with every percent of stock.

- Pass: If the EPS rating is going up, then the inventory passes.

- Fail: If the EPS score is reducing, then the stock fails.

Return on Equity

ROE will inform you how efficiently the control is producing returns.

- Pass: If the ROE has been going up for 2 years in a row, then it passes.

- Fail: If the ROE has long beyond down within the beyondyears, then it fails.

Analyst suggestions

An analyst does quite some large studies on shares after with the intention to provide their recommendation.

- Pass: The recommendation passes if the consensus advice is to shop for.

- Fail: The advice fails is the consensus advice doesn't reap the acquisition diploma.

Chapter 22: Develop Your Trading Plan

A trading plan is the regulations you'll look at on the same time as you are buying and selling. It ought to encompass:

Markets you can alternate on

As a trader, you don't want to limit your self to searching for and promoting stocks. You can pick out out from e-mini futures contracts, alternatives, futures, foreign exchange, ETFs, commodities, and bonds. You ought to study the unique ranges of volatility and liquidity in each of these one among a kind markets. You also ought to come up with a particular plan for each of these markets because a plan for e-minis isn't going to art work properly for stocks.

Primary chart intervals in an attempt to steer your picks

Chart periods are primarily based on hobby, time, or quantity. The one you may choose out have to be primarily based totally for your options and what works for you. No count the chart you select, the price activity will stay the identical.

Settings and signs which you want to exercise to your chart

You will likely study specific technical symptoms and settings for your charts just so they show you what you need to look. Technical signs need to be stored to a minimum, if used in any respect, but you want to determine which of them you need to use.

Your guidelines for position sizing

Position sizing is the greenback rate of your change, and it furthermore works to define the quantity of contracts or stocks you could exchange.

Your access hints

You may additionally both be competitive or conservative as a provider. This is something you could see inside the access guidelines. Conservative shoppers appearance ahead to an entire lot of confirmation, which makes them omit out on trades. Aggressive consumers might be too brief to enter a trade. Setting your recommendations will maintain you from falling into this form of traps.

Your triggers and filters

Thesematters will art work together to offer you your access recommendations. Filters will find out the setup conditions that need to be met to go into a alternate. Once the filters find out it safe to go into, the alternate will then be precipitated.

Your exit pointers

This is the opposite of get entry to. This will ensure that you get out of a trade with as a exquisite deal income as feasible and will hold you from dropping too much cash. There are severa amazing exits you can need to offer you. They encompass:

- Time exits

- Stop and opposite

- Trailing save you levels

- Stop loss degrees

- Profit goal

Now which you understand what you need, you may offer you along with your personal shopping for and selling plan.

Practice Money Management

The following techniques will give you a superb structure to your trading that will help you defend yourself from any vain losses. Utilizing those guidelines will assist save your money.

Wire out

People have a propensity to get excited while their buying and selling account grows, however you could't permit your success go to your head. When you are making big profits in some unspecified time in the future, it's very tempting to try and repeat it the subsequent. Instead, when you have an incredible day, try wiring cash out of your account so you don't lose it. For instance, in case you make $a hundred,000 or extra, twine out$60,000 to $70,000. Those earnings may be blanketed.

Max dollar stop loss

A max dollar forestall loss will can help you apprehend right away at the same time as you're wrong and which you want to get out of your trade. This is going to rely on your account period. If you region your max amount to $500 and in case you are down through using $500, then you have to get out of the alternate right now. Do now not begin trying to rationalize subjects.

No buying and promoting if you could't lose

Don't exchange with cash which you want for residing expenses. You need to constantly ensure which you have coins for bills, food, gas, and exclusive dwelling prices. Anything over that may be used to exchange. You shouldn't assume to lose at the same time as you exchange, however in the event which you do lose, you received't be losing coins that you in fact need.

Chapter 23: Start Paper Trading

You are without a doubt prepared to begin trying out your buying and selling plan and skills. Paper buying and selling approach that you trade without risking any cash. No real cash is used. This will assist you decide out if you will be a success with actual cash or not. While in exercising mode, you want to act the identical manner you may in case you were searching for and promoting with real coins. Don't do some thing out of the regular truely because you could't lose any money.

Before you begin paper shopping for and promoting, you want to do it at the equal tool you will be the usage of whilst you begin stay shopping for and promoting. You need to stay far from portfolio-tracking net web websites because of the fact they don't offer you with everything that the actual marketplace does.

Most brokerage systems may additionally have a demo mode account that you'll be able to access. If you propose on the use of an instantaneous get admission to shopping for and promoting tool like RealTick, additionally they include a simulator mode.

The quantity of time you may devote to paper purchasing for and promoting is completely up to you, further to how long it will take you to sense snug. This must take some days, according to week, or perhaps months, and that's good enough. It's higher to revel in cushty than to emerge as losing all your coins in a unmarried day of stay shopping for and selling.

For proper here on out, you need to spend every single day paper buying and promoting until you sense comfortable sufficient to stay exchange.

Learn When You Should Walk Away

In order to make coins thru day searching for and promoting, you need to recognize even as you need to stroll away. There are masses of professional buyers that exceptional have a fifty four% win ratio. That doesn't imply they don't make coins. This simply method that they revel in some small losses.

This is the most crucial trouble to preserve in thoughts, as you want to ensure that your losses stay small. You should realise on the identical time as you have to walk away. Buying is the quality element you can do. The toughest element is knowing the right time to promote a inventory.

The same is likewise proper for triumphing trades. A lot of consumers will see income, and they count on that in the event that they wait in reality a bit longer, they will get even higher income. The trouble is, they maintain to observe for a danger to make extra and more money, and then they grow to be losing all of it. Walk away even as you meet your get

proper of entry to and exit elements, don't wait.

Gauge the Market

There are severa folks that will stay laser-centered on the inventory they exchange. You want to step again and take a look at the general trend and make certain which you aren't overexposed. Allow the marketplace to manual you.

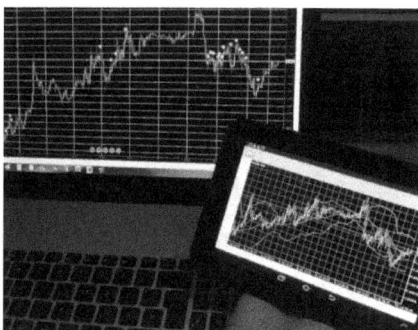

An important difficulty for a dealer to do is to continuously use the market to gauge wherein you want to input and exit stocks. This is one of the fine strategies to ensure which you live normal. This way the style may be your buddy.

A couple of factors to have a look at on the same time as you are trying to gauge the marketplace are $INDU and $IWM. This is only taken into consideration certainly one of many one-of-a-type methods you could gauge the marketplace, and what you select is in the long run what works first rate for you.

Start Live Trading

You've made it to the big day, congratulations.

You now get to slowly begin day purchasing for and promoting. First, you need to make certain which you are extremely good which you are prepared to start shopping for and promoting with real coins. This isn't some activity.

I can't permit you to realize what to do to your first day of stay searching for and promoting. You ought to take into account your plan and strategy, but there are some assets you need to check off your listing in advance than you purchase your first characteristic. Make high-quality you have:

• A brokerage account with the proper amount of charge range

• A purchasing for and promoting plan

• A watchlist of shares

• A charting software application

These are the most crucial topics that you need to ensure you have got have been given before you begin your first day of live shopping for and selling.

Review Your Trades

This want to be completed after your first complete day of purchasing and promoting so you can see the way you in all likelihood did, and so that you can alter matters for the following day of purchasing and selling.

Reviewing your trades is wherein you critique your functionality to conform along with your plan and apprehend how the plan worked. A self-evaluation wants to be completed on every occasion you exchange, and a shopping for and promoting plan evaluation desires to be completed weekly and monthly.

A self-assessment way that you test the trades you made that day and then affirm how properly you stuck in your buying and promoting plan on each of your trades. If you ended up making a number of trades that have been not part of your plan, then you definitely virtually have a trouble. If you notice trades that you should have made constant together together with your plan, then this is additionally a trouble. Try to discover the areas in which you had issues so you can pay near hobby to the ones hassle regions and enhance on them.

Then at the save you of each week and month, you want to go through your charts for every other assessment. Try to find out the regions which is probably causing you problems. What's essential is, you find out the regions wherein your searching for and selling plan failed or times even as you didn't follow your plan for that reason. These are the regions you have to be cautious for and attempt to restore.

Adapt Your Strategy

After you have have been given traded for an entire month, you can begin to make small adjustments in your shopping for and selling plan. You can base those adjustments on the topics which you have determined throughout your overview classes. It's vital that you exercise your modifications to make sure that they'll in reality assist you. Changes want to be made cautiously because of the truth they might turn out to be being premature. You can't make adjustments based totally on a unmarried change. You need to take a look at the overall consequences.

You need to make certain that your plan adjustments live small. You shouldn't overhaul the whole plan. This will will assist you to make small modifications and then check to see if it is actually useful. If masses of adjustments are made, then it is going to be tougher at the way to locate precisely what location wishes to be tweaked. At your subsequent assessment consultation, you'll be able to decide if that exchange helped, or in case you need to observe every other location of your plan.

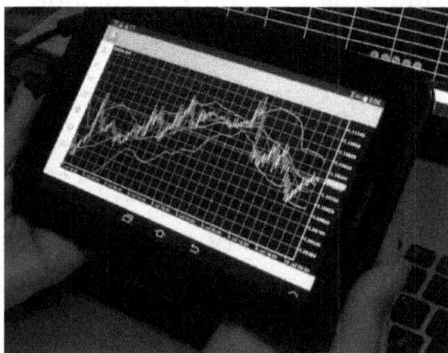

Keep Your Emotions in Check

You should make certain you preserve your feelings in take a look at whilst you are shopping for and promoting, or it can end up costing you large time. Just because of the reality you had several losses in a row, that doesn't mean you may have a losing day. The following 5 recommendations will assist you hold your emotions from ruining your trading:

Walk after every exchange

This might be most effective for a minute. Walking faraway from your pc will provide you with a deliberate spoil from the demanding pace of buying and selling. This will assist you separate your self out of your trades.

Find the least risky hour

Instead of trading at some point of this hour, take a look at a e-book. Your plan will likely paintings better sooner or later of the extra unstable hours, so take a damage whilst your plan is much less probable to schooling consultation for your preference.

Take a ruin after 3 consecutive wins or losses

This method when you have made three wins or three losses. Wins will make you experience invincible, so that you can purpose you to overtrade. Losses will make you revel in like a loser, for you to reason you to 'revenge alternate.'

Stay far from your earnings and loss

While shopping for and selling doesn't have a examine those numbers, wait until the end of the day. These figures may additionally purpose too fantastic of an emotional reaction.

Am I scared?

You don't need to be afraid even as you're making a exchange. If you're scared, then you definitely ought to go out your trade, look over your suggestions, lessen your duration, and repeat.

Stay Consistent

There areforemost things to help you to stay constant: one, your education, work, and behavior, and , your effects. Getting constant outcomes is the made from the proper form of and amount of hard work, training, and method. Make exquisite which you hold your effort regular. You ought to maintain to conform with everything that you have observed inside the previous chapters. There isn't some thing that you can prevent the use of. Continue your every day self-assessment and your monthly plan assessment.

This manner which you moreover need to set apart the proper quantity of time to dedicate to your paintings. Other buyers are handy devoting 60 plus hours every week to studying the markets, gaining knowledge of stocks, and getting prepared. You don't need to slack off and provide them the wonderful trades you could have made.

If you can't commit normal effort and time, then you definately definately want to just walk away. The first-rate issue you may do right now could be to write down down a each day ordinary. Hour with the beneficial aid of hour, realise what you will do every day that you exchange. This way you can set aside time for buying and selling, studies, assessment, and arrangements.

There are masses of factors which you need to do in the course of the day apart from change, so a time table will assist you to stay ordinary. It will hold you from feeling too careworn. And, this may moreover maintain you from feeling scatterbrained and could hold you more targeted.

If you keep on with what you've located out with the useful resource of the use of preserving a regular recurring, and if you follow your plan to the letter, then you will be a a achievement and normal issuer in no time.

Chapter 24: The Basics Of Trading

As you put together to plunge into day purchasing for and selling and start reaping earnings, there are a few essential records that every new day supplier needs to recognize. By know-how those statistics,

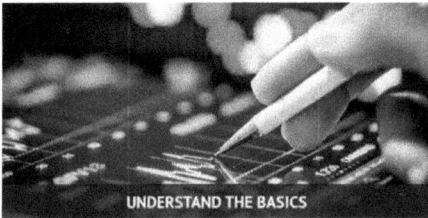

UNDERSTAND THE BASICS

you'll be capable of dispel the myths about day buying and selling so that you can feature in a a success manner.

To start with, here's a evidence of what day shopping for and promoting is not. Day shopping for and selling isn't always a immoderate-risk approach of being worthwhile, wherein you can lose lots more than you benefit, especially within the quick run. Neither is day buying and selling a get wealthy quick scheme, wherein you may double your capital if it's miles significant enough—specially if you are hoping to achieve this internal a month.

Day buying and selling is often assumed to be easy, with someone sitting in the front in their pc and playing with numbers. It is far from easy or smooth; in truth, it calls for training and method to get it proper. Finally, day buyers are not a gaggle of kooky folks who are their personal logo of loopy. A day dealer is a person which includes you, who has recognized the way to spot and capitalize on an opportunity.

Day Trading and Gambling

For some years, day searching for and promoting acquired a lousy rap, mainly because it turned into being abused. Gamblers, as an example, have been trying to day buying and selling a terrific manner to get their repair. When you undergo in mind the chances in gambling and those in day shopping for and selling, you will be able to see the obvious versions.

In gambling, you are more likely to lose out, especially because of the truth the possibilities are never in fact to your select. With day looking for and selling, this isn't always the case. What is wanted rather is right planning, and one can be successful.

Beware of Your Capital

In the method of pastime looking for and selling, you may turn out to be with an unlucky situation. That is one in that you lose the whole thing, all of the capital that you had invested. If you are seeking out a manner to develop your cash and have positioned your profits into an account for day trading, you have made the wrong selection and will with out issues become destitute. What one need to do is commit a few cash to day trading, after which overlook approximately it in phrases of applicable use.

This does not take a look at with you, the usage of your discretionary earnings; it simply refers to your risk capital. Risk capital is in reality cash that you may now not mourn over need to you lose it. You ought so one can control to pay for it being long gone.

Day Trading as Business

Should you've got were given made the selection to go into the arena of day buying and selling, you need to understand that day trading is a profession or a career choice—it is not some difficulty that you do for a laugh on a Sunday afternoon as you'll do with a hobby.

The purpose is easy. Day searching for and promoting requires an investment in time to learn how to get it proper and the development of skills. It additionally requires an extensive plan, everyone who's in search of to discover day buying and promoting as a interest will in all likelihood lack the time to create a plan.

You May Get Lucky

As a brand new dealer, you could accumulate a go to from girl achievement and make a great amount of money out of your very first exchange. Though this can be amazing for you, and will clearly constructing up yourself warranty, ensure which you hold to artwork for your destiny successes. If you aren't cautious, you can lose all of your success (and your coins) on your one-of-a-kind trades.

If you possibly did show up to be fortunate, do now not take it as a one off. Take the time to investigate and recognize what exactly you likely did to purpose such an top notch return. If you can retrace your steps, it makes it less difficult to apply this method to destiny trades, and optimistically, keep the same momentum.

Choosing a Market

Variety is the spice of lifestyles, and on the equal time as you start day buying and selling, it'll appear which you are spoilt for preference. But even spices include wonderful warmth meters, and also you want to be careful to choose out one which you can stand. This is the same as deciding on a market. Here are some of the factors that you need to preserve in thoughts.

• Whether you're in relevant economic fitness. This has a critical function to play on the form of marketplace that you can have interaction in.

• The electricity of your person and your custom shopping for and selling device. The markets are a hard area to be, and in case you do no longer have a thick pores and pores and skin, you could locate that they may with out issues break you. You want to learn how to pick your battles so you get closer to achievement.

• Your area geographically. You may discover which you are restricted to best a positive variety or shape of market.

When you're selecting a marketplace, you need to recognize that as a amateur, you'll be higher relevant for positive markets, on the same time as as an skilled day supplier, you can have sufficient talents to choose some factor a hint riskier. Beginning buyers have to start by way of manner of choosing a market that has minimum margin necessities, low tick values and is shifting at a medium pace. This will make certain which you are not left placing with now not whatever to expose to your efforts.

Defining a Hot Tip

When it involves day shopping for and selling, there may be quite an alternate of records, specifically records that is meant to assist with profitability. Most buyers are aware of warmth recommendations, which promise that during case you take a look at them, you can make a killing. These kinds of guidelines are frequently communicated thru the grapevine and they could first-class be defined as rumors.

The purpose that they may be so undercover within the way that they're surpassed on, or maybe from the person who is imparting the statistics, it that during case of any troubles, it is the supplier who is probably responsible.

Should a day dealer acquire a warmth tip, which elements within the path of some information this is valid, they could have an unfair advantage. This technique that distinctive human beings strolling within the equal vicinity have to enlarge terrible relationships or outlooks toward that specific day supplier.

Insider Trading

Insider buying and selling is slightly one-of-a-kind from getting a warmth tip despite the fact that the manner that the facts is conveyed to personnel might be very similar. It is all about finding underground strategies to bypass the records in advance. It is basically any facts that has now not been made public, which can be used for the motive of securing a sale. Insider education will usually be passed in advance via someone whose opinion is excellent in a specific location, or who works inside the place and has come to be privy to some new modifications.

There are dangers for day consumers who act on insider trading tips. These are typically penalties which is probably imposed need to one be determined with this data. If you have got been to make the most of the insider shopping for and promoting records, then the penalty may be three instances the quantity of your profits and if the authorities decides that as a issuer, you have got been indulging in crook behavior, the penalty can be even better.

The assignment with insider looking for and promoting is that it is difficult to prove, as maximum of it takes place with word of mouth, so there can be no paper path. In addition, pretty some the so-referred to as guidelines that are given out as insider looking for and selling often become completely baseless.

Chapter 25: Basic And Investment Strategies

The use of an effective manipulate machine in your cash can start to help you cultivate wins even if you quality have four trades which may be worthwhile out of the 10. So, take time to workout, then plan, and ultimately shape the threads that you do in step with the manipulate of your coins and the allocation of your capital plan.

Consider the charges that the brokerage could be charging you. When day trading, you will see not unusual transactions as a way to consist of consequences of appreciably costly brokerage charges. Once you have got carried out your studies very well, you may be in a position to devise the right brokerage company that you may go through a carefully idea after plan. If you want to nice alternate one or regular with day, then you may want to find a provider that charges on a in step with alternate basis plan. If you are planning to do day shopping for and selling, then your quantity goes to be excessive. In this example, you want to go together with a staggered fee plan. The better volumes which you have, the lower the fee will efficaciously be. You also can advantage from a plan that is a constant rate. This will provide an limitless amount of trades for one high constant price.

Trade Management and Position Sizing

Apart from all of this, the supplier moreover offers services that embody utilities for trading and structures that you can make use of for buying and selling. The included solution for buying and selling can be topics together with mixtures options, software program searching for and selling, information for historic accuracy, equipment that help with research, indicators for the trades, programs that chart with indicators which can be technical along thing capabilities that are not already listed. Some of these abilties may be rate-powerful or loose, on the identical time as some may also encompass a fee that could devour a hollow to your profits or pockets. You must choose the capabilities which might be available for your shopping for and promoting desires and keep away from those which is probably subscribed to assist with particular desires. A novice can begin with easy low-price brokerage costs that match the buying and selling desires which is probably to start with set, and then later, they could select modules and upgrades which is probably wanted proper now.

You can even want if you want to simulate or contrary take a look at the historic information of the strategies and buying and selling charts. Once you have were given got set a plan and it is prepared, then you definately genuinely need as a manner to simulate it to test the technique and utilize the take a look at to run a digital take a look at account with virtual cash. Many of the dealers that you can hire will allow you to run a check for your account. You also can use the historical information to lower again take a look at the technique. This will offer you with an assessment that is practical, in addition to preserve issues for the price of the brokerage and charges that in the end will arise for the best of a kind diverse utilities.

Strategies

For maximum people, techniques are applied in organizations to offer industrial corporation operations a sense of course. However, maximum people neglect about about the fact that techniques are an essential part of our regular lives. They assist you to stay your lifestyles so as and accumulate even the pleasant of dreams. Basically, any journey undertaken with out a technique does now not have an actual blueprint for addressing the severa factors of the adventure.

The significance of doable strategies cannot be underestimated almost about day trading. They shape the framework under which the marketplace may be studied, and investors leverage the maximum profitable possibilities of making earnings. In all day shopping for and selling strategies, there may be a need for in-depth technical assessment to installation the forms of the charge movements via charts and the specific signs for one-of-a-type strategies. The basic guiding precept of an afternoon shopping for and promoting approach is that emotions must be out of the method development way. Every approach selected should be primarily based on facts, and there are various factors to be taken into consideration at the same time as selecting any method.

Trading Based at the Time of Day

Often, this critical assessment goes to be stored for prolonged-time period making an investment, a few factor which you don't see lots with day buyers. It takes under attention how the rate of the agency will skip into the future even as compared to in which it's miles now, however those adjustments are regularly going to stand up over weeks, months, or perhaps years. Day buying and promoting takes area in at some point. Because of this, maximum day buyers will not use this facts to help them make alternatives approximately which stocks to change in.

As a day provider, you possibly acquired't spend a whole lot of time strolling on crucial research. Most consumers realize that a call for in ethanol goes to make a distinction inside the price of corn at some stage in a particular time period. But day traders need to reputation more on what the rate is going to do right now in assessment to wherein it come to be a couple of minutes within the beyond.

Chapter 26: How To Develop Your Own Strategy

For new investors, it is probably suitable information to pay attention that there are numerous day buying and selling strategies that you probable can adopt. You can pick out to observe books along with this or take guides that may educate you at the great techniques which you could adopt. Regardless, it's far critical to understand that trading may be a DIY career. Most successful consumers develop techniques which paintings for them. As such, constructing your non-public technique have to constantly be part of your interest. In line with this, you shouldn't be glad that constructing your personal method is a difficult undertaking. In reality, while you get right right right down to organisation, you will be conscious that it's miles quite straightforward. This challenge rely will take you through the fundamentals of developing your very own day shopping for and selling technique.

Market Selection

With the arrival of on line shopping for and promoting, this has made it possible to have a large range of monetary devices that buyers can depend upon. In this case, humans can alternate on other monetary devices besides stocks, futures and options. Recently, there have been one-of-a-kind trading alternatives, which includes the Foreign Exchange Market (FOREX), Single Stock Futures (SSF) and Exchange Traded Funds (ETFs).

It is nicely actually well worth putting forward that the present economic securities have been superior to embody virtual contracts of exquisite commodities collectively with natural fuel, gold, silver, grains and crude oil. These futures have emerge as well-known each day amongst day shoppers. It is because of this that pit-traded commodities have been overtaken through the excessive quantity of mini and virtual contracts.

Essentially, the net has made it viable to change on anything. Take, for example, actual estates, it's far feasible to go into this organisation with out in reality proudly proudly owning any homes. This is made feasible thru Real Estate Investment Trusts (REITs). To apprehend how you could choose out the fine marketplace to alternate, it is vital to study the precise markets in my view. There are numerous markets which you may trade in. However, we'll interest at the most famous, together with shares, futures, forex and stock alternatives. These markets can be scrutinized based totally on capital requirements, leverage, liquidity, and volatility.

Capital Requirements

One of the primary problems that maximum traders would possibly bear in mind is the quantity of capital that they require to initiate their buying and promoting pastime. Therefore, it's miles honestly nicely really worth analyzing the markets based totally totally on the quantity of capital that you may require to start day trading. Often, expert shoppers will recommend the concept of beginning small and growing step by step. This gives a amateur trader enough time to research and master the paintings of day looking for and promoting.

Leverage

Another vital problem to mull over is leverage. After understanding the way to alternate on considered one among a kind markets, a issuer may want to commonly make the brilliant out of the little capital they are the use of to exchange. In this case, leveraged markets deliver them the possibility of maximizing their income by using the use of certainly the usage of a small quantity of capital. Consequently, the benefit obtained within the utilization of leverage is that a small account may be advanced rapid.

Liquidity

Understanding markets based mostly on liquidity is essential. Focusing on liquid markets warrants that buyers avoid the common market troubles of slippage and manipulation. Undeniably, any trader may also want to make sure that they achieve correct fills for their orders.

Volatility

Without volatility, it might be no longer possible to make cash from distinct markets. Therefore, markets need to be moving for people to make cash. In relation to this, know-how the most volatile marketplace guarantees that a provider places their cash in possible markets.

By now, you need to be curious to apprehend how markets vary. The following paragraphs will communicate vital facts about the only-of-a-kind markets you may turn to available. Undeniably, expertise is power. Hence, understanding what to expect from the ones markets is important for any supplier.

Selecting a Trading Timeframe

Obviously, day trading could require you to pick out a time body, this is an awful lot less than a day. It is well really worth noting that the time you pick out out may additionally have an impact on the earnings you're making. For example, if you choose a time frame it is lots plenty much less than 60 minutes, the probabilities are that your income may be decrease. If you change the use of a bigger time frame, it's going to growth your possibilities of getting greater earnings.

With smaller time frames, you get smaller income. Nonetheless, the advantage here is which you decrease your risks too. This way that during case you're new to buying and selling, smaller time frames might be a smart preference. There are professionals and cons to brief and prolonged-term frames. You in reality need to make a choice primarily based absolutely to your financial desires. The exceptional manner to make your preference is thru experimenting with various timeframes. If your method doesn't art work with a small time frame, you could switch to a bigger time frame.

Defining Your Entry Trigger

Besides facts the proper market to trade in, you furthermore mght need to recognize even as to go into the market. Candlestick and bar styles are perfect triggers to apply. The following photo suggests you processes the triggers will appear to be.

Knowing Your Exit Trigger

Certainly, with day searching for and promoting, something can move wrong. There are instances while markets will speedy drop, that could have an impact on your returns. Knowing even as to exit is, consequently, crucial. Essentially, exiting isn't just about promoting at the identical time as topics don't flow your way. You moreover need to go out while matters are going as you predicted. This ensures that you make the great from your funding. You should usually set your feelings apart due to the fact the market will now not always be for your side. Know when to save you at the right times.

Define Your Risk

After knowledge at the same time as to go into and exit the market, you want to understand how a great deal hazard you may stomach. The tremendous manner of doing this is through position sizing. Position sizing lets you comprehend the quantity of coins you're ready to chance. If you double your position length, it way that you may additionally double your hazard. Always ensure that you make a decision your feature period as it should be.

Know Your Trading Rules

At the begin of your buying and selling interest, you'll be conscious that the buying and promoting rules you use are simple. In reality, you could memorize some of the ones rules. Regardless, it's miles endorsed that you write your rules down. This is a sensible method which ensures you hold situation within the course of your buying and selling interest.

Constantly Improve Your Trading Strategy

Your searching for and promoting technique will now not normally deliver you earnings. This is regular thinking about the fact that your approach is not static. As you hold buying and promoting, you may advantage understanding and experience. Therefore, you need to find a manner of moreover enhancing your looking for and selling method. When doing this, you need to, however, alter the method regularly and no longer drastically.

In a nutshell, having a purchasing for and promoting approach is vital for the fulfillment of your buying and selling industrial enterprise. You ought to strive to apply a shopping for and promoting approach that you are snug with. With regards to choosing the right marketplace to change, furthermore make sure which you make your preference based in your financial goals. Don't definitely choose a marketplace because of the fact most humans are shopping for and promoting there. Your selection want to be primarily based completely mostly on what you watched works for you.

Chapter 27: Ideal Tools And Software

Just like another business organisation, day buying and selling furthermore calls for a bunch of gear. You need a provider and a reliable looking for and selling platform to

kick off your adventure. Some of the favored device you could have already got. Currently, buying and promoting has lengthy lengthy long past digital and masses of traders have get admission to to monetary markets internationally via the net. It is always an splendid concept to hold a smartphone in case you want to talk for your dealer. You may also even want a computer and a pc. I will offer an cause of detail about what form of tools you need for the adventure and why they will be vital.

The Tools

The smooth tool is your laptop. Technology is changing in a fast manner, that's why you want to make sure which you have a computer that has enough memory and a quick processor that doesn't lag continuously or crash in the center of the art work. Most of the shopping for and selling software application application require rapid processors that could wrap up obligations . The 2d maximum vital tool is the software program application you operate. Most dealers offer plenty of software program alternatives that you could use. This software program program has the number one hobby of tracking the fees of economic belongings. Day traders generally need to apply the software software program that could permit them to apply considered one in all a type charts like timed charts and tick charts.

Ninja Trader is a famous software that you could use for charting and buying and promoting. Different brokerages are well matched with one in every of a kind software program program software. The fact stays that you're going to want an fantastic broker in your buying and promoting ventures. A correct dealer is your key to a profitable alternate. With a horrific supplier, you could lose money. Many dealers are amazing and that they have tremendous software software application. Their rate structures are also notable. However, a few are cheap as nicely. You want to undergo the net in advance than you pick out out out the issuer to your investment ventures.

Remember that each provider will offer you with spherical 3 to 6 times, leverage in your funding. If you make investments round $30,000 on your purchasing for and selling account, you may have $100 and twenty,000 searching out energy. That's a leverage of 4:1. In not unusual trading language, leverage is referred to as margin. You have complete rights to exchange on margins, however you ought to be answerable for it. It is fairly smooth to buy at the margins however is also easier to lose on the margins. If you lose, your supplier takes the loss from the precept capital you had invested in the account. That's the purpose you need to be in session with the trader over how plenty margin you must set. Margins can divulge you to greater risks.

Margins work without a doubt as mortgage does for your home. You borrow a huge amount of cash and then purchase your house. Banks will provide you with a loan, however they won't take the duty or hazard over the equal. If you placed $100,000 and borrow $900,000 from the economic group on a loan, this makes a 10:1 leverage to shop for a $1,000,000 house. If the rate of the house jumps as plenty as $1, hundred,000, you continue to owe the financial group the authentic $900,000 and the interest. The income you have got made has come from the leverage that you had been furnished. You couldn't have sold the residence if it were no longer for the leverage. If the charge drops to $900,000, you owe the financial group $900,000 and the hobby. This drop in fee has price you $100,000, this means that which you have lost all the particular down rate.

Keeping in view those conditions, you should pick out out the dealer that is nicely disciplined so that you should get hold of a margin call on each change you're making on leverage. A margin call is much like a vital warning. Day traders ought to keep away from receiving those margin calls. A margin call method which you must upload more money to your account otherwise your broker will freeze your account.

The buying and selling platform has the equal amount of importance. Fast execution of trade is the important thing to a a achievement day buying and selling profession. Just don't forget that you want to region orders in a unmarried minute and the shopping for and promoting platform hangs up for the subsequent 5 mins or the shopping for and promoting platform is truely too gradual to load up in split 2nd. If your supplier doesn't have a quick software program application or shopping for and promoting platform that runs on hotkeys, you want to do not forget converting the dealer. You virtually actually cannot get the quality information of the trades in a quicker way. When the stock's rate spikes, you need so you can positioned coins on your pocket with the useful aid of selling it real short. You will no longer need to be fumbling to find your orders. Quick execution is the important issue right here, that is why I suggest which you rent an green company that focuses on and guarantees actual fast alternate execution.

The Trading Community

Trading is a fancy commercial corporation. It isn't always any easy feat and isn't for the prone-hearted. You want to be emotionally robust as it is able to get emotionally overwhelming for you. Therefore it's far continually the best way to sign up for a buying and selling community and ask them approximately their studies. You can communicate to them and observe new strategies of purchasing and selling and techniques. You can have lots of indicators and tips approximately the inventory market. You can chat in a non-public chat room collectively along with your near buddies and own family people as well. When I traded, I remained in communication with my pals at the smartphone. We intimated every unique approximately the possible fluctuations within the charge. We additionally shared facts opinions, technical assessment, charts and graphs via emails to maintain our community up to date. This helped us keep time. This furthermore saved us from frustration as well that originated from lack of awareness. Some purchasing for and selling systems offer live chat carrier to buyers as nicely.

If you be part of a cutting-edge chat room, you may talk to skilled buyers as properly, who might offer you the right advice on the lowest of revel in. You can request them for tips and pointers of day buying and selling. You can often art work on developing your network or you may be a part of an already established community. Creating and growing a community is unfastened.

Online Trading Tools

All depending upon the gadgets that you want and your degree of experience, there are a few tools that you could get proper of entry to online and use to make your buying and selling agency famous.

• Trading View

This is one of the top well-known charting systems that you can access on line and use for giving a lift for your searching for and selling business. It generally covers all markets the world over, along side indices, foreign exchange, shares, and futures, and so on. This application permits you to software a customised script. It additionally gives you an entire lot of signs that permit you to share charts with the buying and selling network you have got were given developed or have joined. It is free to join up at the platform.

You also can take unfastened membership, which offers you advanced functions.

• Stock Charts

Stock charts' crew is the pioneer in stock buying and selling. They had been around for quite a long term and they offer severa charts together with Line, Point & Symbol, Candlestick, Renko and Ichimoku. The most exciting component about this platform is that you can see the general price regular performance of the inventory over a specific duration. For instance, you may degree what turn out to be the proportion whilst it closed the final January. It additionally tells how a good deal higher or lower it modified into from the present day price.

• MT4

If you are a forex provider, you could probable have heard about this well-known platform. You or a number of your friends have in all likelihood been using it already for doing business business enterprise inside the

the Forex market market. Many brokerage agencies offer CFDs devices on MT4. The great aspect approximately MT4 is the level of response that it gives to its clients. There is type of 0 lag time if you hop from one chart to each unique. If you are a swing or a characteristic holder, you would love this platform.

Chapter 28: Do-It-Yourself Risks

Risks are a part of stock making an funding or any investment. You can not keep away from these risks, no matter how knowledgeable you're. The best way to deal with these risks is thru manner of minimizing your publicity to them. Before you can boom techniques for minimizing your risks, apprehend them first. You want to apprehend an appropriate sorts of risks and what elements have an impact on a danger to end up a threat to your probabilities of incomes gain.

The Different Kinds of Risks

Risk is dropping detail or all the charge of the investment. Some dangers are without delay associated, while exceptional risks in a roundabout way affect stocks investment and your searching for power. Risks are inherent to any investment, so do not allow those dangers avoid you from investing your cash on stocks.

- Financial Risk

Financial hazard is a assignment even for set up organizations. This threat refers returned to the lack of ability of a organisation to pay its buyers. Remember, a agency that publicizes insolvency can pay first the creditors before paying shareholders and investors whilst the organisation is in the technique of liquidation. More regularly, shareholders won't recover their investment fee while the company announces financial ruin.

• Risk Related to Interest Rate

It is used to expose the effect of a hike in interest charge after buying an investment. Oftentimes, this form of danger is immediately related to investments that generate jail responsibility or investments that require price of interest payout to investors. An instance of prison duty-generating investment is bonds. Interest charge danger affects the economic scenario of a corporation, in particular for agencies that rely on debts gadgets to raise capitalization.

This threat impacts stock investment. When a business corporation issues bonds and unique money owed devices and suffers from surprising progressed of interest charges, probabilities are their capability to pay might be affected. Higher fees imply better rate of interest. This manner the enterprise can pay first the lenders earlier than they'll pay their traders. As a give up result, the price of shares may additionally decrease or dividend payout may be postponed.

With a better interest charge, stock buyers will be predisposed to sell their stocks, specifically within the electric and economic industries. These traders also can decide to invest in debt devices in vicinity of inventory funding. To lessen hobby risks, expert customers diversify their portfolio with the useful resource of creating an funding in coins market devices that carry out and however earn even all through immoderate-hobby prices.

• Market Risk

Market danger refers to the demand and deliver movement in the marketplace. When a kind of percentage turns into in demand and its supply will become constrained, its rate will increase. Conversely, when no investor desires a specific stock, its price decreases. Price and fee of stocks growth or decrease depending on market name for. This is the purpose stock is a risky investment in a quick-time period length. The inventory market is unpredictable due to the tens of thousands and thousands of buyers shopping for and promoting stocks in an afternoon. One minute, a stock's rate boom. The subsequent minute, the same inventory's rate crashes because of the truth no person decided to shop for it. Aside from the call for, distinctive elements may also have affected the rise and fall of a stock's fee, which includes the economic situation of the issuing organisation, political and governmental state of affairs and inflation.

The component, do not invest your cash in stocks if you do now not apprehend what you are coping with. Ignorance can deliver you huge losses.

•   Inflation Risk

Inflation danger refers to the lower in shopping for energy an investor has. You can't purchase the identical object on the equal price and the same quantity compared years within the past. For instance, you can purchase 10 sweets with a greenback 5 years in the beyond. Today, you may still buy the same emblem of candies with a dollar, but the amount decreases. Perhaps nowadays, you may simplest purchase five or lesser.

How does this threat have an effect on your inventory making an investment technique? Suppose you buy a stock that yields 4% payout and you make investments the rest of your cash in the monetary institution that earns 4% interest. In effect, you are earning. Your first funding might be at threat with the need growth in hobby price and financial condition of the issuing business enterprise. Your second investment is stable and isn't at chance with a better interest rate. Since you've got invested the relaxation in a financial institution, your cash earns anything interest that the financial institution uses.

However, the inflation price is spherical five%. Your profits are under the inflation rate. This technique your funding inside the economic company is losing cash.

- Tax Risk

Tax threat is the lower in what you may get. The cause of inventory making an investment is to construct wealth. When there may be wealth, a tax is present. You need to pay a detail for tax duties. This way you want to be informed on tax so you can keep away from paying extra taxes than you earn.

- Political Risk

Sometimes, whilst the government problems new hints and policies, some groups are affected. Others may also even grow to be bankrupt because of a particular law, at the equal time as some organizations may additionally additionally additionally benefit from this same law. In a poisonous and unfair political surroundings, companies may moreover die or live. Thus, it does now not damage if you have a smooth know-how of the manner politics paintings in nations due to the reality political and governmental conflicts may have an impact on a commercial enterprise corporation's financial circumstance. In a few countries, corporations may want to probable grow to be political goals.

• Personal and Emotional Risk

Personal chance refers to your disability to increase your investment whilst an opportunity arises. This can also discuss along with your disability to keep an investment due to the truth you need coins right away.

The first state of affairs arises when you have sufficient cash to make investments however are afraid to shop for more. Alternatively, it is able to be that you do not have the cash due to the fact you've got spent it in an emergency. The 2nd state of affairs arises whilst you do now not have an emergency fund to pay on your emergencies. The first issue you need to do is making sure that you have an emergency fund on the identical time as you start inventory making an investment. If you bypass that step, you are much more likely to revel in those conditions ultimately.

Emotional risk refers to your loss of potential to govern emotions at the same time as you decide to shop for or sell a stock funding. Most of the instances, many shoppers allow their emotions control their rational wondering. In stock making an funding, you are both grasping for more or be afraid to lose cash. These are excessive feelings which you want to discover ways to manage whilst making an funding in stocks.

- How to Minimize Risk

Stock market making an investment may moreover include such a whole lot of risks, but minimizing such risks is straightforward and viable. Don't let those dangers prevent you from making an investment. Risks must not be your predominant criterion in locating out whether or not to invest or now not.

- Stop, Gather and Learn

Before making an funding your cash in stocks, gather as an entire lot information as you can control. Learn the whole lot you need to apprehend about stocks making an funding. The extra statistics you understand, the more is your hazard of creating and selecting winning shares. If it takes you years to understand even the number one language of inventory making an funding, so be it.

The essential component is minimizing dangers of losing cash right into a undertaking you recognize no longer anything about. Indeed, you would possibly argue that the first rate teacher is professional, but it does no longer suggest you need to stand a struggle without making organized for it. If you determined you aren't organized, then don't begin searching for stocks no matter the insistence of a monetary adviser. Financial advisers may be professionals in their subject, but they'll be now not the ones who will undergo the loss.

• Remember the Basics

Whenever you revel in strong enough to combat, always keep in mind the basics. Make advantageous to keep your self grounded and continuously pass decrease lower back to the basics of inventory making an investment. These number one mind allow you to collect your desires with out losing a huge amount of cash.

• Diversification

This refers to a mix-and-in shape method in inventory making an funding. You don't focus on one funding. Your portfolio consists of short-term, intermediate and prolonged-term investments. The percentage is predicated upon to your private style of investment. If you're an competitive investor, the bulk of your funding coins is positioned on brief-term and intermediate investments. A lesser percent is on lengthy-time period investment. If you are a conservative investor, maximum in all likelihood, a big bite of your investment cash is positioned on lengthy-term investment. Only a small percentage is on quick-term and intermediate.

Another way of diversifying is with the resource of the use of making an funding your cash in specific financial gadgets. Do not concentrate your investment cash on stocks on my own for the cause that inventory marketplace is a risky marketplace.

www.ingramcontent.com/pod-product-compliance
Lightning Source LLC
Chambersburg PA
CBHW071218210326
41597CB00016B/1866